Gemstone Journeys

Also by Shelley Kaehr, Ph.D.

Books:

Origins of Huna: Secret Behind the Secret Science
Lifestream: Journey into Past & Future Lives
Galactic Healing

Videos:

Gemstone Journeys
Stones of Power

CD's:

Origins of Huna: Ho-Oponopono Cord Cutting
Journey to Spirit: Meeting Your Guides
Journey to Spirit: Abundance
Sacred Sound Healing
Lifestream

Original music by Christine Cochrane

These titles are available from Galactic Healing.
Visit the website at www.galactichealing.org

Gemstone Journeys

Shelley Kaehr, Ph.D.

SECOND EDITION
First Printing 2002

Edited by Linnea M. Armstrong
Cover design and photos by Mitchael Kaehr

Library of Congress Control Number:
2002094981
Kaehr, Shelley A., 1967—
              Gemstone journeys/
Shelley Kaehr - 1st ed.
              p.   c.m.
              Includes bibliographical references.
              ISBN 0-9719340-1-0

    An Out of This World Production does not participate in, endorse, or have any authority or responsibility concerning private business transactions between our authors and the public.
    If you wish to contact the author or would like more information about this book, please write to the author in care of An Out of This World Production and we will forward your request. Please write to:

Shelley Kaehr, Ph.D.
c/o An Out of This World Production
P.O. Box 610943
Dallas, TX   75261-0943

www.outofthisworldpublishing.com

*When man first
entered this plane,
it was not in a
physical form.
He entered as a soul,
a spiritual entity,
in which there was
embedded a spark
of the Divine Fire.*

Edgar Cayce

Acknowledgments

As with any endeavor of this magnitude, it would not be possible without the love and support of many people.

First, to my parents, Mickey and Gail, for giving me the upbringing that allowed for gemstone explorations to occur on a regular basis.

To my brother, Mark, for always being a willing participant in my experiments.

To Joe Crosson for your love and friendship and total belief in my cause, I owe a debt of gratitude. Thanks for attending my very first gemstone healing class!

Special thanks to Linnea Armstrong, my editor and lifelong friend. Without you, there would be no *Gemstone Journeys*! And to David, Connor and Ashlyn -thanks for making me feel like part of the family!

To Christine Cochrane - our creative synergy is one of the greatest gifts I have in this lifetime.

To Cheryl Doyle - thanks for all your help!

To Gary Fleck and Kayse Williams. Your work is an inspiration.

To Katchie Stewart of Raiders. Thank you for being my friend and teacher.

To Charlie Mark of Mountain Mark Trading, I thank you for introducing me to Larimar, which I consider to be the greatest gift of the mineral kingdom.

To Gregg Braden, I thank you for your support and friendship. Your work is an inspiration.

Finally, to my students for your willingness to explore the wonders of healing gemstones.

Contents

Part Two: The Stones

Part Three: Healing with the Stones

Dance of the Rays

(Radiance)

Thoughts and feelings of "Christalline"
(crystalline) light
stirred the ethers...

Swirling, scintillating, intricate colors
and lattice grid forms interface - allied...

Solidity

Angelic dreams manifest

Proof against time

Nocturnal

Present...
CRYSTAL

Gary Fleck 2002

Introduction

I believe some of us were born loving rocks and minerals. My love for these treasures of the earth was nurtured by my parents, two avid "rock hounds." My mother majored in geology in college; my dad managed a Turquoise mining company in Arizona when I was a child. We spent our family vacations hiking, hunting rocks, and panning for gold in the mountains of southern Colorado, and they taught me at an early age to seek out rocks—first for personal companionship, and later for healing and medicinal purposes. I began to see rocks not only as souvenirs, but as friends.

This book details my lifelong journey with the gifts of the earth and the discoveries I have made of the healing potential within the mineral kingdom.

This is by no means a complete look at all

the earth has to offer in this capacity. It is merely a compilation of my experiences and those of my clients, who have greatly benefited from the various stones we will discuss.

One of the challenges of writing a book such as this one is that each author has his or her own experiences with various stones, used individually and in combination. Each person must experience the stones firsthand and experiment to see which stones resonate with their particular energy.

I have often asked myself whether or not gem healing is for real. Do the stones actually heal people, or is it merely the energy and intent we put into the stone that causes the favorable outcome? I will explore this phenomenon in greater detail throughout the book.

We are all natural-born healers. I hope this book encourages you to get in touch with that lost part of yourself and helps you begin to tap into your innate gifts. Just as each stone is unique, so is each person, and this book is intended to serve as a "tour guide" for each reader's individual journey. Exploring the healing powers of the mineral kingdom is a fun process of self-discovery. I wish you a joyful journey.

Part 1

How's and Why's of Gemstone Healing

One
My Journey with Healing Stones

Since I have been around stones and spent time in mines for many years, I am sure I benefited from the healing effects of stones even as a child.

It was not until later in life, though, that I began to consciously consider that not only were the stones energetically appealing, but that each could be used to alleviate or enhance various states of consciousness.

My journey with gemstone healing began when I befriended a powerful Native American shaman who introduced me to the process. He instructed me to lie still, then placed a magnificent piece of frosted green Fluorite on my forehead. At first, nothing happened, but he insisted I continue to lie still.

About five minutes later, I began to feel a

surge of energy rush through my body down to the soles of my feet. I could not believe it!

After that experience, I immediately began experimenting with other stones. I spent hours taking notes on the effects I felt from each new one.

Eventually, I developed a fairly substantial body of information and was asked to teach a class at a metaphysical shop near my home.

The class was so well-received that people who were not there that day asked me to teach it again. I decided to teach the class in my home and to invest in some inventory. Over the years, the class became very popular and my quest for knowledge greater. Now, I feel the time is right to publish my discoveries in a book.

My prayer is that this book will be read by people who may or may not have experienced the wonders of stones, and that it may inspire the reader to follow up on some of the ideas I present here. Mother earth has so many wondrous gifts for us if we will take the time to seek them out and appreciate them. I believe the healing gemstones of the earth are among her most amazing accomplishments.

The information here is *not* meant to replace the wonders of modern medicine, which at times is absolutely necessary. Gemstone healing should be seen as a preventive measure to stop illness before it starts and as a healing aid that can be used to enhance any medical treatment an individual is currently using. I believe medicine is a great way to put out a fire once illness has already developed. My goal is to help you avoid the doctor and maintain a state of excellent health and mental peace.

Two
Why it Works

The fabulous book *Vibrational Medicine* by Richard Gerber, is, I believe, one of the best at explaining how and why crystal healing works. In the book, Gerber explains that according to physics, all matter in the universe is vibrating. There could be no universe, no planets, no Earth, and no you and me if there was not first a sound vibration that created everything. Students of Eastern philosophy believe this sound is "Om."

Each sound has a unique vibration. Think of a bass guitar: remember how, after a chord is struck, you can actually *feel* it inside your body? Here's another example: have you ever been sitting in your car stopped at a railroad track as a train went by and felt the rumble of the cars as they drove past? Both sounds had vibrations, and both not only sounded, but also felt, different. That's what I mean by vibration.

Everything is made up of these sound vibrations and of particles of matter called atoms. The frequency and pitch of the sound determines how the atoms are put together. If you are sitting in a chair right now, it is interesting to contemplate that you and the chair are actually made up of the same matter, yet you are put together differently. Of course, you have the added component of consciousness, but let's forget about that part for a minute and concentrate only on your physical body.

Before you were created on the physical plane, an energetic blueprint of you in perfect health was created as a mold for your physical form to be "poured into." (Picture a cement worker pouring cement into a mold.) Your body, composed of atoms, was scheduled to be "poured into" its perfect mold so you could be at peace when you got here.

It is interesting, however, to observe that when your body is created, it often misses the mark of perfection and winds up having a few less-than-perfect parts. It's as if you have "built-in" energetic blockages when you arrive, rendering it impossible to pour you perfectly into that mold.

Why would that happen? I believe it

happens because if things were perfect, we would not have anything to learn here. We all came here to learn and to slowly, over several lifetimes, grow into a being more closely aligned with our "blueprint of perfection." This "blueprint" is also known as our etheric double.

The blockages we're born with could come in many forms: karma from our past lives; trauma or stress from our current one; or thoughtforms, which is a term used to describe the energetic component of simple thoughts.

It is my observation and opinion that crystals and gemstones heal us because they act as a bridge between the perfect state of health enjoyed by our etheric double and the current state of our physical bodies. Tapping into the perfection mother earth has created allows us to tune our bodies in to this perfect state, thus effecting healing in ourselves and in others by allowing the stones to assist us.

Three
The Spiritual Bodies

The energetic part of you is something you may not have considered before. A good example of this is if you have ever been to a funeral. When I go to a funeral, I find myself gazing into the casket, looking down on my friend or loved one and thinking "That's funny! Bob's body is there, but *he* is not there!" Many of you know what I am talking about.

That is the big question of life—where did "Bob" go? The energetic component, or soul, has gone somewhere else. While we are on the earth plane it is important to realize this part of us is real and must be cared for.

This spiritually perfect part of you waiting to be tapped into is made up of several components. These components are often explained by the theory of the three spiritual bodies: astral, mental and causal.

Astral Body

The astral body is the energetic layer closest to your physical body. It is the place we speak of when we describe "astral traveling" and it is where you may often go in the dream state to meet with other souls or to work on more mundane tasks.

If you have ever experienced déja-vu, that feeling of familiarity when meeting someone or visiting someplace new, that is often because you have been visiting that person or place via the astral plane. This is different than past life recall. Let me share a personal example.

A couple of years ago, I had an amazing opportunity to go to Greece. I have always felt that I lived in ancient Greece in a past life. When I arrived in Athens, I immediately fell in love with the place. Strangely, though, I found all the houses and buildings of modern Athens to be amazingly familiar. Everything appeared exactly where I believed it should be, and I had an incredible innate knowledge of the city's geography.

How could that be, I wondered, if I had only lived there during ancient times? My theory is that I had been astral traveling to Athens in my dream state, which would explain why I knew my way around town so well.

My brother tells some amazing stories about this very activity. At night, he says he consciously travels out the ceiling of his bedroom. When he was in high school, he decided to visit his band hall at 6:30 a.m., well before anyone arrived at school. He said the room was still, and he could see the sheet music and everything as if he were standing there in the flesh.

Another amazing story of this phenomenon comes from a friend of mine who, as a child, would astral travel to visit her father while he was out of town on business trips. Her father was often awakened by her presence and could actually see her standing at the foot of the bed. He would call her mother at home the next day, and to everyone's amazement, he would describe the pajamas his daughter had worn the night before.

I received an interesting piece of advice from yet another friend, who warned me never to astral travel without my clothes on. He claimed he accidentally astral projected himself into a friend's bedroom some 1,600 miles away and was seen naked! Fortunately, in this situation I doubt you could be arrested for indecent exposure!

You are probably engaging in astral activities, too, outside of your conscious awareness. Some people theorize that as you dream, anytime you consciously remember yourself in the dream-state looking out of your own eyes, as opposed to watching yourself as if you were part of a movie, then you are actually engaged in an event on the astral plane.

So the next time you see someone who appears familiar to you, ask yourself if you have encountered this person on the astral plane. If the energy or soul of the person seems familiar, then you may wonder if you encountered that soul in another lifetime - interesting questions to ponder.

Mental Body

I used to think the mental body was all about thinking and brain power, until my guides recently explained fully what the mental body is all about, and thanks to their help, I have discovered that there is much more to the mental body than I originally thought.

I have several steady clients who have seen the benefits of energy work and come in regularly to be balanced.

When I get the opportunity to work with people regularly, the benefits can be amazing. It is with these individuals that I have begun to more fully understand the subtle energies of the human body.

When a client first comes in, I usually spend time clearing energetic blockages on the astral level because that layer is closest to the physical body. If left unattended, these blockages could theoretically lead to illness and discomfort sooner than blockages that are further out in the auric field.

One particular client would come in every week. During each visit, my guides instructed me to do something completely different that was for his highest good.

One day, after I had been working on him for quite some time, I was given clear instructions that we were working on issues regarding manifestation. I was asked to use specific stones (which we will go over in detail later in the book) to create the energy necessary for him to receive abundance. I was also instructed to work on the mental body with the stones.

On most people I have encountered, this layer of energy is about six to eight inches above the physical body. We manifest and create from the mental body, and the energy here allows abundance to flow to us. Creative endeavors such as writing, painting or music are also manifested in the mental body. Blockages in the mental body literally block our creativity and hinder our ability to attract abundance.

Causal Body

The causal, or spiritual, body is the part of you that is connected to the lifeforce, or God. This is the spiritual self—the soul.

All illness has an emotional or karmic component. Before illness ever manifests itself on the physical plane it is created out in the causal body.

Illness is a gift. It represents that which you came here to learn—the reason why it is first created on the causal level.

On my own journey, illness played a major factor in my willingness to explore and learn about gemstones and energy healing. I see the illness as a gift from which I was able to learn in order to follow my life's purpose.

Many people hang on to illness, as I once did. That in itself is a powerful lesson. Why we do or do not heal is intimately tied to our karmic lessons in this life. It is not a judgment of "good" or "bad"—it is simply how we choose to learn.

causal

mental

astral

The Spiritual Bodies

The power of crystals and gemstones in healing at the causal level is stunning because the crystal can facilitate your lessons for you without your actually having to manifest the illness on the physical plane. Crystals can cut years and even lifetimes off the learning curve.

Four
Stones and the Chakras

In addition to the three-layered subtle energy system described above, we have another subtle energetic system called the chakras. The chakra system responds not only to sound, but also to color and to the vibrational frequencies of the colors of the spectrum.

If we were actually able to see the chakras, they would look like colored tornadoes, beginning at the base of the spine and working up to the top of the head. Generally, the lower three would swirl in a counter-clockwise direction, and the upper four would rotate in a clockwise direction.

Root

The root, or first, chakra is located at the base of the spine and vibrates to the color red.

When functioning properly, this chakra keeps us grounded in earthly activities, and helps us feel centered and connected to the earth. If we are feeling "spaced out," confused, or disconnected from reality, there may be a blockage there.

Sacral

The sacral, or second, chakra vibrates to the orange color frequency and is located just below the navel. The creative part of the person, as mentioned in my discussion of the mental body, is located here. It is the part of you that is able to create and manifest. The second chakra is also our sexual center.

The healthy functioning of the first and second chakras combined enables us both to create and to actually finish things and bring them out to the physical plane. An example of someone with a well-functioning second chakra is a musician who writes her songs, then actually completes the album and takes it to the marketplace.

A blockage in this area could mean someone is lacking financial abundance, or is incapable of finishing a project.

There can be unhealthy over-activity in a chakra as well. A woman with an over-active, unbalanced second chakra may have reproductive problems.

Solar Plexus

The third chakra, or solar plexus, is located at the convergence of the ribcage. It vibrates to the color yellow and is the seat of our personal power. How we stand up for ourselves and demonstrate courage are the lessons imparted by the solar plexus chakra.

I am fascinated by the work of Carl Jung and others on the collective consciousness, the idea that when humankind as a whole thinks about certain universal truths, we create huge energetic representations of these thoughts in the universe in the form of astral matter. According to the theory of collective consciousness, that matter affects all of us on a daily basis.

Another theory I once heard is that humankind as a whole operates in one of the seven chakra centers at any given time.

It is believed that before the fall of Atlantis that we were evolved to a very high level, but that after the great destruction we had to start from scratch and work our way back up.

We began with the root chakra, or the basic

survival instincts. When we collectively moved into the sacral chakra, we became more occupied with the sexual side of our nature. At this time, we began to see diseases that reflected that consciousness—such as AIDS—pop up.

Many theorists feel that during the '90's and until the tragic events of September 11, 2001, we concentrated on our manifestation of material possessions (a second chakra function) and moved into power trips centering on money and ego, which are all about the solar plexus.

Heart

The fourth chakra is the heart. It surprises many people that the heart chakra vibrates to the color green, since we often associate it with rosy red or pink. While these colors are also very healing to our hearts, it is actually the healing green of Mother Nature herself that resonates with our best heart center.

Many believe a shift in the collective consciousness is presently occurring and that humankind as a whole is beginning to shift to the heart chakra.

The process of shifting is not always easy, as evidenced by the many people suffering from various heart ailments and diseases. Since heart disease is still the number one killer in the United States and other nations, it will be interesting to observe the changes that may occur over our lifetimes as we successfully shift our attention to love and away from greedy materialism.

Lessons of the heart deal not only with loving others, but with loving ourselves as well—not an easy journey for many of us.

Throat

The fifth, or throat, chakra is light blue and is all about communication. By "communication," I mean how we speak our truth in the world.

Many people are stifled by others' negativity and by a fear of expressing themselves. As we are able to accept ourselves more and to share our ideas and personal truth as we see it, we open our throat chakras.

I can attest to the fact that this area has been a lifelong challenge for me, as I am sure it is for many others. Because we live in a society where "political correctness" counts and lawsuits abound, it is easy to see why communication is an issue facing mankind on a large scale.

Many of us, myself included, also have a

desire to want everyone to like us. Sacrificing our true thoughts, emotions and feelings for silence so that people will like us is an issue of the throat. The throat chakra challenges us to have the courage to be ourselves.

A good example of someone with an open throat chakra is a singer, because it takes a lot of courage to get in front of others and sing. Likewise, professional speakers and actors are also more likely to have opened the throat center.

Third Eye

The third eye is the sixth chakra, located on the forehead. This is our mystical, psychic, intuitive center, and the one chakra many of us would most like to open.

The third eye chakra vibrates to the color of indigo, a purplish blue. Those who have clairvoyant visions, or who seem to predict the future, have opened the third eye.

This is not a privilege reserved for the few who inherited the ability at birth. With diligence, anyone can develop this gift.

The third eye also represents the intellect and truth and involves the eyes and ears, brain and the pineal and pituitary glands.

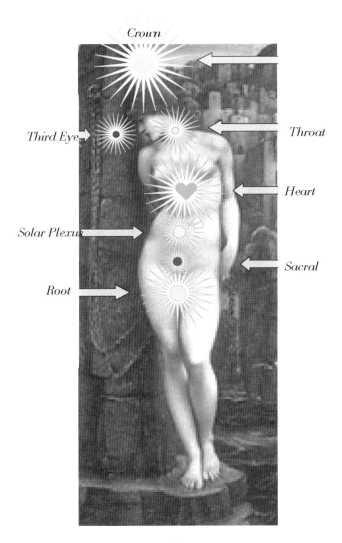

Crown

Third Eye →

Throat

Heart

Solar Plexus →

Sacral

Root →

Gemstone Journeys

Crown

Five
Selecting Stones

The question students and clients most often ask me about stones and crystals is, "which one should I take?" The answer is simple: whichever one you pick up first—whichever one you are attracted to.

The Rolling Stones' axiom, "you can't always get what you want; you get what you need," is so true. It is my opinion that the first stone you pick up is *absolutely, without question,* the stone you need.

Even among stones of the same type, individual stones are like people: each has its own unique energy. Just as individual members of a particular race have differences, so do the stones.

The process of selecting what you energetically need at that moment *should* be left to your higher self, or unconscious mind. It knows the answer and often easily chooses something.

The universal laws of attraction are interesting to observe, though, and they are easily recognized when someone is selecting a stone.

Invariably, a crystal shopper will pick up the stone he needs first. Then, he usually begins to analyze the other stones. In doing so, he sometimes selects another stone he deems more attractive.

As you can see in the example above, it is often at this point in the process that the plague of humanity—the *ego*—steps in. The ego is much more interested in looks than in substance and is interested in that which is most physically attractive. It is at this moment in the selection process that many of us are subjected to "bait and switch," because the ego mind wants the stone it thinks is prettier, lighter, heavier, or somehow better.

It is simultaneously interesting, amusing and frustrating for me to watch my students engage in this battle—and watching someone pick a stone is definitely a metaphor for the battle between the ego and the higher self.

I must admit I find myself falling for the ego's line at times. In fact, it happened to me just recently.

I was making my annual pilgrimage to the Loretta Chapel in Santa Fe, New Mexico. The Loretta Chapel is the famous chapel containing a spiral wooden staircase that has no nails holding it together.

Legend has it that in 1887 some nuns needed a chapel built on to a girl's school and called in a local artisan to do the work. When it was completed, it was discovered that the man had inadvertently forgotten the staircase to lead to the second floor. The nuns began to pray to St. Joseph for help when one day a stranger came to town and offered to do the work. Six months later he disappeared without a trace leaving behind the stunningly beautiful seamless staircase made of wood not indigenous to the area.

Loretta Chapel is one of my favorite places on earth. It is a beautiful place charged with immense spiritual power. I purchase my holy water there and usually like to get something from the gift shop.

As I walked through the gift shop on this particular visit, a crucifix "called" to me to pick it up. I read the label and discovered it was actually handmade in Bethlehem.

It was not very expensive, so I decided to get one. Before I knew what was happening, I found myself rummaging through the other crucifixes to make sure I had "the best one."

I forced myself to stop and to take the one I originally picked up because I consciously remembered what I just told you. Energetically, I needed the first crucifix I picked up for some reason that may be totally outside of my conscious awareness.

I often feel the need to gather items from various parts of the world, regardless of whether I have actually been to that place. Different geographical areas have unique vibrational qualities; this is another form of subtle energy we can tap into. In the case of the crucifix, I feel my guides were urging me to tap into some Holy Land energies, perhaps due to all the conflict going on right now in the Middle East. A very effective way to heal an area is to concentrate on it in prayer. Having energetic matter from that particular place on hand can be very powerful.

The story of my crucifix shopping experience is a classic example of the struggle between the wants of the ego and the voice of the higher self. Learning to listen to that voice is a major undertaking, but it is something we all need to work on during our lifetime.

Here is an important point to consider when collecting stones: each is truly one of God's unique creations. There is no stone exactly like yours anywhere, nor will there ever be. When we find a stone we love that loves us back, the special relationship is a unique gift from Spirit that should not be taken for granted.

So in the final analysis, always go with your first instinct. If another stone—or whatever it is you are selecting—seems more attractive, buy it also if money permits, but don't leave without the one your soul was first attracted to.

Six
Cleaning Gemstones

Stones are made up of energetic matter, just like you and I, and just as we are affected by the emotions—both positive and negative—of others, so are our stones. As such, they need to be cleansed.

Earth

To me, the best way to clean the stones is to place them back on mother earth, where they came from, so they may be nurtured and healed directly by their source. Of the many cleaning methods I have tried, this, to me, is what feels both most beneficial and most appropriate.

The best way to do this is to place the stones directly on the earth itself. Then, if need be, use distilled water to rinse off any dirt after cleaning. (The chemicals in tap water can negatively affect your stones.)

If this is not easy to do or you are in a rush, as I often am, place them on the patio or concrete walk so they may still receive grounding, yet not need as much time for rinsing, and so forth.

Salt

I mentioned earlier that we are affected by the energies of others. This is the case partly because when our subtle energy system is functioning well, it can create an energetic ball around our bodies of up to 27 feet. Under normal, day-to-day circumstances, that energetic part of us is about three feet in diameter around the physical body.

What this means to us is that when others pass close to us, they are actually walking right into our aura! As such, it is easy for us to pick up other people's "stuff," both positive and negative.

In crowded areas, the mass consciousness alone—even if everything is positive—can be enough to wear you down.

The best example I know of this is in the shopping mall. Imagine yourself as if you are just a golden ball of light 3 feet in diameter and when you walk through a mall, people are literally walking right through your auric field! Plus the masses of people and the frequency of florescent lighting can all wear you down if you are not careful. Personally, I avoid the mall at all costs!

I go to quite a few metaphysical expos and shows, and I do energy healing work on a lot of people during the course of a day. It quickly became important for me to find a way to easily cleanse my auric field.

I have found that the best way to do this is to use sea salt or Epsom salts in the bath. Salt is an amazing substance because no negativity, or low vibrational matter, can penetrate its barriers. It can instantly cleanse your auric field of any blockages so you feel like yourself again.

I have recommended salt baths countless times to people who visit my booth at these shows—people who ask for my help because life has become such a burden, with caring for others, stress at work, and the like, that they feel they cannot go on.

I cannot think of a more effective, inexpensive way to rid yourself of many of life's burdens than by going to your local grocer, investing in a $1.99 carton of Epsom salt, and spending even 15 minutes submerged in the bathtub.

Many of the things bothering you right now have nothing to do with you! It's true! It is the energy of other people!

This information changed my life! I recommend the Epsom salts because, as I said, they are so inexpensive and easy to access. Sea salt is wonderful, but it costs more. In addition, not everyone has a good health food store nearby, nor do they want to go hunt for one.

Humor me and try this! I promise you will be a believer!

Why do I bring this up in a book about gemstone healing? The point is, if *you* benefit from salt, so do many of your stones and crystals.

For the stones, though, I recommend sea salt first and foremost, especially if the stone in question comes from the sea; to them, it is like going home and they love it.

If you cannot get sea salt, put the stone outside on the ground first. If that is not possible due to living circumstances (for example, if you live in a high-rise apartment building), then use a very diluted Epsom salt solution.

Do not use table salt! It has a different molecular structure and can do more harm than good.

The only time I use table salt is when I am salting the perimeter of my yard. I do that not only to keep the slugs away, but also because, as I mentioned before, nothing negative can penetrate its protective shell. Among salt's amazing healing powers is that it keeps the home safe from others' negative thoughtforms and from psychic attack, where another person willfully sends ill will toward you.

Some of you reading this now may likely question the validity of what I am saying here, because you may not yet be consciously aware of exactly how others' thoughts affect you. Over time, I have come to be a big believer in the fact that many of our illnesses and non-karmic energetic blocks are actually caused by people sending thoughtforms to us. When these thoughtforms are sent with harmful intent, this action is defined as a psychic attack.

I want to be quick to stress, however, that not all negative thoughtforms we receive are the result of psychic attack. Someone may simply be thinking something negative in general and your auric field may accidentally get caught in the line of fire.

We must remember that thoughts are things! They take up space. We must develop the self-discipline to begin "policing" our thoughts and to heighten our awareness of them—because thoughts create.

For every action there is a reaction; that is the basic definition of karma. Along the same lines, every thought is a creation you put into the universe. It will affect something somewhere. Be careful what you create!

Now, back to the salt: it's a cleanser that will repel negativity and, therefore, cleanse you and your stones. It is a powerful and affordable tool.

Sage and Smudging

One of the best ways to cleanse space and stones is with a sage wand, also known as a smudge stick.

Native Americans use the technique to cleanse the auric field of the body and sacred space.

The wand looks like a bundle of dried sage leaves or grass that can be lit to cleanse the air in a space, or in this case, it uses the element of fire to cleanse the auric field of the stone. In the next chapter on elixirs I will discuss how this works in

You simply light the wand with a match and you should see a substantial amount of smoke emanating from it. Then, with pure intent in your mind and heart, pass the stones through the smoke while keeping thoughts of cleaning and purity in your mind.

I have also used another version of the sage method by making a pot of sage tea.

I had a very special Amethyst stone I used to use in almost all my healings that had been damaged by the sun and had faded to the point that much of the vital force had been sapped from it.

I took some sage spice like you get at the grocery store and boiled it in a pot to create some sage tea.

It is important to wait until the brew cools down or it will damage the stones, so after the tea had cooled, I soaked the stone in it for a few days and it brought back some of the original luster, although it was never the same again.

Damaging Stones

This brings me to an important thing to consider: stones can be damaged by overexposure. Obviously, stones are of the earth and therefore it is usually acceptable to keep them out in the elements

Several stones can become damaged and will fade when exposed to the sun.

This seems to be particularly true of some of the quartz family and stones that are naturally occurring underground. Some of the more sensitive stones include: Amethyst, Fluorite, and Rose Quartz.

I enjoy cleansing my stones in the sun and moon, particularly during the light of a full moon when energies are strongest. At times, I would put some of the more sensitive stones out overnight, planning to bring them in first thing in the morning. I would often get busy and forget to bring them in and that is when my Amethyst I mentioned was damaged. So learn from my mistake and use care when placing precious gemstones in the elements.

Seven

Elixirs

Gem Elixirs

This topic is one of my favorites to cover. It is exciting to witness the effectiveness of gem elixirs.

At the beginning of the book, we talked about our etheric double, or the energetic portion of us in perfect health. Physicists think of this as a "hologram" of sorts that each of us has.

Furthermore, if we are all one (as I mentioned before), and if we are all part of the energetic "stuff" that makes up the universe, wouldn't it make sense that everything in the universe would have a hologram of its own—that trees, animals and plants would all have a hologram of perfection energetically linked to them?

Dr. Edward Bach discovered this in England as he experimented with his well-known flower essence formulas. Bach realized that dew drops collected from various plants and flowers could be used in formulas that would create a variety of positive results in people. Bach used the plants' dewdrops because the etheric blueprint of each species was found in the drops, and they proved to be powerful healers.

Gem elixirs work the same way. Instead of using flowers, though, we are using stones. Gem elixirs allow us to capitalize on the perfection of the crystal's etheric double, and to tap into the perfection of that crystal in our own bodies.

Just like most things, crystals are not always "perfect." Although their molecular structure is quite orderly, they are often clouded, and are then, themselves, in need of healing.

When we use a clouded crystal for our own healing—as I often do—the crystal clears up as it heals the recipient. It is as if the crystal had karma and that helping us enables it to heal itself and to create dharma by doing good works.

To make a gem elixir, soak a crystal in

water and put it outside so it may be charged with the healing life force of the sun and moon. The assumption is that the crystal's blueprint of perfection is soaked off into the water. When we drink the elixir some hours later, it causes physical shifts in the body as it heals our own molecular structure and aligns it more closely with that of the crystal.

You should keep the water outside for at least 24 hours to get the energies of the sun and the moon. If you are in a rush, just put it out as long as you can, preferably in the sun so the water can be charged faster. Unless the moon is full, the sun tends to charge the water faster. Full moon water is a real treat, though, so try it sometime!

Be sure to use distilled or purified water and *always* use a glass jar or container. Chemicals and impurities found in plastic will leach out into the water, which is why you must use glass.

I give a gem elixir made with a simple Quartz crystal to my students, who report feeling an immediate charge from the energy of the water. Though I have always used a plain Quartz for my elixir, feel free to experiment with many different types of stones. Be sure to exercise caution and that the stone you choose is non-toxic. I recommend using only very hard stones that are insoluble in water for this process.

Color

Elixirs can also be made with color. You can, for example, make "green" water. I have done this many times and it is really interesting.

The process is basically the same as that for making a gem elixir: put some distilled water into a glass or crystal container, then place it in the sunlight. The color comes from wrapping the container with colored cellophane. If you want green water, for example, wrap green cellophane wrap around your jar. After leaving it out for 24 hours or so, take it in and drink it. It definitely has its own unique flavor, and each one is different.

Use colors that correspond to the chakra you are trying to heal. Green water would heal the heart or any heart-related conditions. Red could be used for grounding or the blood; yellow, for stomach problems; and orange, for digestion concerns.

Try it! It is really interesting and the water tastes delicious and natural!

Part 2
The
Stones

Eight

Turquoise

Chakra: *Throat, overall healing support*
Chemical Composition: *Copper Aluminum Phosphate*
Found In: *Arizona, China, Tibet, Argentina, Brazil, Mexico*

Because this book is about my personal journey and self-discovery through the stones I have worked with, I feel compelled to list them in the order in which I discovered them; therefore, I will talk about Turquoise first.

"Turquoise" literally translates to "Turkish stone," referring to its original trade route to Europe via Turkey. This stone has had the most lasting impact on my life of any stone to date.

I lived in Albuquerque, New Mexico, in the '70's, when Turquoise costume jewelry was the big craze all over the country, but particularly in the Southwest. In fact, in that part of the country it never went out of style. Even today, seeing Turquoise takes me back to that part of my childhood and the stone has an amazing healing effect on me.

My dad worked for a company that manufactured 75% of all of the costume jewelry seen at trading posts and gift shops. Pieces made by this company are still available today. During this time, my dad befriended many Native Americans, who taught him how to make jewelry. He still makes stunning jewelry using all sorts of stones.

Later, we moved to Phoenix, where he took the job with the turquoise mining company I mentioned at the beginning of this book. Growing up around the mines was an amazing adventure—and quite an education.

Opposite Page: Beautiful piece from Arizona (top), samples of some of the newer Chinese Turquoise (center), The bottom photo shows the way Turquoise is formed by layers of sediment flowing down between layers of rocks.

The Turquoise most of us are used to seeing is deep blue and shiny. When it comes out of the earth, Turquoise is usually light blue or green. The more greenish versions occur when more iron is present in the matrix. Iron is an element of grounding and protection, so if you seek more of those type qualities, you may prefer a more greenish piece of Turquoise.

A lot of the Turquoise in the stores today comes out of Tibet or China. To me, it looks almost plastic—very different from what came out of the Arizona mines I was around as a young girl.

There is a reason Native Americans have made the Turquoise such an important part of their spiritual practices, aside from the obvious fact it is found in our country.

We keep returning to the subject of vibration. Each stone, in addition to vibrating at a color frequency, also possesses a numerical frequency.

According to Melody's book *Love is in the Earth*, Turquoise vibrates to the master number of 55. Thus, its frequency is high, and its atoms are moving quite rapidly. Typically, the higher the vibrational rate, the easier it is for a stone to remove blockages from the subtle energy system and to be of great benefit in healing. Turquoise's high vibra-

Top: Sleeping Beauty Turquoise from Arizona
Bottom: From a mine in Kingman, AZ

tional rate places it in this category.

Because Turquoise is found in colors ranging from blue to green, this stone can be used to open the throat and the heart, and can provide overall healing support based on the theory of the color system and the chakras.

I have used Turquoise myself by laying it on my stomach to receive all over healing support. I describe the treatment and how long to do it in part three of the book.

Nine

Iron Pyrite

Chakra: *Root, Sacral*
Chemical Composition: *Iron Sulfide*
Found In: *Southern Colorado, Arizona, Illinois, Pennsylvania, Spain, Italy, Norway*

I include Pyrite here primarily because it was always one of my favorite stones growing up. I believe it is a favorite of many children because it is so much fun!

Pyrite, generally referred to as "Fool's Gold," is an iron sulfide. It's found in the form of shiny gold colored cubes, or large granular lumps. It got the name "Fool's Gold" during the Gold Rush era of the Old West because it was often mistaken for gold by novice miners who would find it in rivers and/or mines.

Spiritually speaking, I believe it is neat that kids are so attracted to it because it provides some of the very best protection around, and helps keep them safe and sound. It also stimulates the imagination and helps them tap into who they may become when they grow up.

When we are kids, the games we like to play and the scenes we act out during play are often our soul's way of offering us hints about our life's purpose. Unfortunately, many of us are discouraged from following our dreams by adults who have yet to achieve theirs and who do not want the children to be "disappointed."

It is easy to see why they call it "Fool's Gold!"

Pyrite allows us to reach our highest potential, and to have fun doing it!

Ten
Tiger's Eye

Chakra: *Solar Plexus, Third Eye*
Chemical Composition: *Silicon Dioxide*
Found In: *South Africa, California, India, Australia*

Another favorite childhood stone of mine was the Tiger's Eye. The stone got its name from its looks—it really does look like the eye of a tiger. This wonderful stone continues to be one of the most popular stones of our lifetime.

Tiger's Eye's most common naturally occurring color is yellow/gold. The red and blue versions of the stone are artificially dyed, yet can achieve good results when applied to specific chakra centers that resonate to the color of the dye.

As an adult, I was most fascinated with the blue and red versions for a change of pace because the stone has been so familiar to me throughout my life.

Tiger's Eye is a warrior and has deep Native American energies. It is one of the most powerful protection stones available, as it relates to gathering courage. Its yellow color resonates with the solar plexus region, which is the seat of power.

This photo shows the difference between red Tiger's Eye (left), blue (center) and yellow (right). Only the yellow is in it's natural state. The others are dyed!

I have found the blue version helpful with activation of the third eye, and the red stone centering during meditation. This could be due to the color frequency.

As the name suggests, the stone can aid physical vision by healing the eyesight, and spiritual vision by opening one to clairvoyance and prophecy.

Eleven
Rose Quartz

Chakra: *Heart*
Chemical Composition: *Silicon Dioxide*
Found In: *Southern Colorado and throughout the United States, Brazil, Madagascar, India*

Rose Quartz is very prevalent in the mountains of Southern Colorado, and was a gemstone my family hunted a lot when I was growing up.

All members of the Quartz family are composed of silicon dioxide. Quartz is actually a Slavic word meaning "hard," and Quartz got its name because it is, indeed, very hard.

The Rose Quartz is a wonderful stone bearing

amazing healing potential. Backed up by the clear frequencies of the Quartz family, its pink color is particularly healing to the heart. It can be used to activate and balance all of the chakras and provides excellent overall healing support by transmitting feelings of love—both for oneself and for the universe as a whole—to various ailing parts of the body.

People who meditate with the Rose Quartz will appear more attractive to others. That could be romantically attractive as well as in other ways, for example in business situations. It also aids users in building strong rapport with others. I believe its effectiveness comes from the fact that when we are heart-centered and loving, all things are better.

When used as an elixir, Rose Quartz's high vibrational frequency may also promote weight loss, and it is even said to remove wrinkles! It sounds too good to be true! With all this going for it, I am surprised the planetary supply hasn't been tapped out already!

When I feel my clients have any situation relating to their emotional health—such as a broken heart or a grief-related issue—I always have them hold a piece of Rose Quartz. I believe it acts with the unconscious mind to set our intent to heal at a deep level. In my healing practice, it has also been

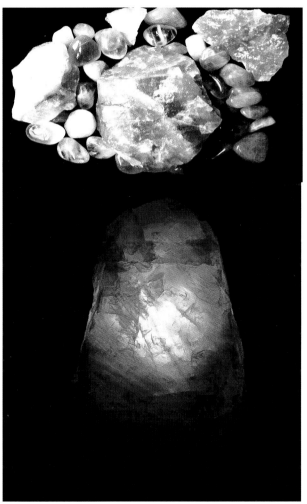

Rose Quartz lamps are very healing because the frequency of the pink light is soothing to the system.

very effective.

When I personally need a pick-me-up in the late afternoon, I often meditate with Rose Quartz because it is wonderful for giving energy to the body while opening the heart center.

Of all the stones I discuss in this book, I think Rose Quartz is one of the most important stones to have on hand. It is inexpensive, easily accessible and very healing.

Twelve
Amethyst

Chakra: *Third Eye, Crown*
Chemical Composition: *Silicon Dioxide*
Found In: *Southern Colorado, Arizona,*
Brazil, Uruguay, Canada, Mexico

      The other stone we used to hunt when I was young was the stunning southern Colorado Amethyst, the best-loved member of the Quartz family. It is the carrier of the purple color ray of the spectrum; therefore, it activates the third eye and the crown quite effectively.
      Purple is also the color of trance, so in my private practice it is a good stone to use for regres-

sion clients because it can be very soothing and will assist people in going into a hypnotic state.

Like Turquoise, Amethyst is a stone that looks completely different depending on where it is found. The variances are found in the depth of the color as well as in the size of the points.

Colorado Amethysts have beautiful big points and a lighter purple color, while Uruguayan pieces have tiny points and are such a dark purple they can appear to be black. Brazilian pieces, which are now the most common, are medium in color and point size and are also quite stunning.

Amethyst is an activator for both the crown and the third eye. Its particularly high vibration makes it useful for all sorts of ailments where blockages need to be removed. This could include headaches, swelling and overall healing support.

I always run a stone back and forth over a client's auric field during a session, and Amethyst is a stone I use at some point in most healing sessions. It has a very high vibration, and I have found it to be very effective in removing blockages and giving clients an instant energy boost.

In my classes, I always use the Amethyst to demonstrate aura cleansing because it is so effective, inexpensive, and easy to find.

A little-known fact about Amethyst is that it

was one of the most revered gemstones of the early Christian church.

The name "Amethyst" is Greek and means "not drunken." For this reason, it has been noted to be effective in treating addictions. When I work with a client who is suffering from alcoholism or any other addiction, I often have them hold a piece of Amethyst to aid them with any shifts in consciousness they are attempting to make.

Amethyst is a stone you should definitely work with as you advance on the spiritual path.

Previous page photos:
Top: Colorado Amethyst
Center: Brazilian and Arkansas samples
Bottom: The rich dark Uruguayan Amethyst

Thirteen
Hematite

Chakra: *Root*
Chemical Composition: *Iron Oxide*
Found In: *Lake Superior USA, Tennessee, Canada, Brazil, Venezuela*

Hematite is the magnetic lodestone (actually, these two terms are synonymous and refer to any stone with magnetic qualities) that absorbs negative energies and provides protection and grounding to those who use it. It forms near lava deposits and is considered to be the most important planetary form of iron.

I was introduced to Hematite by a Wiccan friend of mine when I lived in Colorado. At the time, I was going through a divorce and had just been in a car accident. Everything around me seemed to be swirling in all directions in a chaotic and dysfunctional manner.

I told my friend I was having a bout of "bad luck" and asked for her advice. She told me to purchase a Hematite necklace or ring and wear it all the time. She explained that the stone would absorb whatever was coming at me and that my luck would inevitably change as a result.

I bought a gorgeous handmade Hematite necklace from an African art gallery owned by a friend from South Africa. When I told him the reason for my purchase, he was quite curious to see whether it would work for me.

The necklace was strung on a heavy wire and had a barrel clasp. It was extremely substantial. I put it on immediately and did not take it off at all.

I noticed that I felt much better when I wore the necklace. Soon after I bought it, I purchased a few pounds of Hematite from a mineral shop and kept the stones in a bowl in my apartment.

I was home one day about a week later when suddenly, the string of the necklace dramatically broke and the beads flew all over my floor. I could not believe it; as I said, the materials used to make it were quite sturdy.

You may have seen the Hematite rings currently being sold in all the gift shops. Several people have reported to me that after a period of wearing their new rings, the rings actually cracked in two and had to be thrown away. That happens because the jewelry was not grounded.

Another interesting story about Hematite comes from a friend whose husband was unemployed for several months following a corporate downsizing. She became concerned about his emotional state and bought him a piece of Hematite to absorb some of the negativity she believed was swirling around him.

"I gave him the stone at 2:30 that afternoon, and he put it in his pocket and carried it around," my friend said. "By 10:00 the next morning, the stone was already cracked."

These stories shed light on one of the keys to caring for Hematite: it does absorb negativity, but can only take in so much before it cannot stand it anymore, and it simply breaks. Hematite must be grounded by placing it outside on the ground so the negative "vibes" it has received will be absorbed by the earth.

This quality makes Hematite an excellent fertilizer for your plants and trees. Just as manure is "negative" matter, yet produces growth in plants, the negative vibrations of the stones produce a similar result. This is caused by a magnetic force and is a great example of yin/yang energies.

Hematite is one of the most powerful protective stones available, and it is also easy to obtain.

Fourteen
Fluorite

Chakra: *Third Eye*
Chemical Composition: *Calcium Fluoride*
Found In: *Brazil, Tennessee, Southern Colorado*

At the beginning of the book I told you that my first actual healing experience involving a gemstone was with a beautiful piece of green Fluorite. Since that initial experience, I have continued to use Fluorite quite often and find it to be one of the most powerful stones I have ever encountered.

The stone comes in green, purple and clear. It is often called Rainbow Fluorite because a single stone can have all three colors occurring in amazing patterns, similar to that of a rainbow.

When I work with this stone, I keep in mind the color of the particular piece I am working with and place it accordingly on my body. For example, I tend to use the green version more with the heart chakra and the purple with the third eye and crown. Melody calls Fluorite the "genius stone" because it allows the user to concentrate and to learn complex subjects. I have extensive personal experience with this concept.

When I was in school, I would study every day. I tend to get tired around mid-afternoon, so each day I would place Fluorite all over my body for about 20 minutes or so—just long enough to take a reasonable break.

The power of Fluorite is unmistakable. After my "power nap" (as I would call it), I was able to get back to work without becoming dis- tracted and I absorbed the material much more easily. It seemed answers to questions literally popped off the page.

Because it has an uplifting effect similar to that of the Quartz family, Fluorite gave me the energy boost I needed to get through the day. I then experimented with it on my eyes and ears.

I tried this because my eyes were tired from reading. I had no idea of the actual benefit of doing this, but soon noticed rushes of healing energies in my eyes. Now, after using it for quite a while, I no longer need my glasses!

Although my hearing is exceptional, I found that putting Fluorite in my ears (use extreme caution if you try this at home!) seemed to help clear my sinuses, which usually cause problems for anyone living in North Texas. That discovery led me to begin using Fluorite on my actual sinuses, which are located under the eyes. I noticed immediate improvement as my sinuses seemed to drain and find relief from the process.

I began trying this out on clients when they came in for energy work. Without exception, those who suffered from allergies—including puffy eyes, headaches and ear infections—benefited greatly from the use of Fluorite.

Many of my clients who buy it for their own personal use are able to use Fluorite quite effectively on their own, regardless of whether they had any formal healing training.

Fluorite is both one of the most powerful and one of the most attractive stones around. It's a great addition to any set of healing gemstones.

Fifteen
Citrine

Chakra: *Solar Plexus*
Chemical Composition: *Silicon Dioxide*
Found In: *Brazil, Madagascar, Argentina*

Citrine is actually a member of the Quartz family. It is most closely linked to Amethyst, because it is created by heating Amethyst. Citrine rarely occurs naturally.

Citrine's name is similar to the word "citrus," which is implied by the stone's lemon yellow color, which comes from iron. When Amethyst is burned down, it creates a gem formation that is a golden, yellowish white with little bubbles and inclusions in it. The process also creates one of the most amazing healers on our planet.

Citrine is the carrier of the yellow color ray and, therefore, activates our solar plexus. We may use it to feel powerful and to tap into our personal power.

Anytime we need to feel powerful— whether in a business meeting or to ward off people who continually attempt to violate our boundaries— Citrine allows us to learn how to do that. It can help you stand your ground.

Citrine is also one of the only gemstones I know of that never needs cleaning. Its unique composition does not allow negativity to penetrate it, which is one reason it is such a special stone. Like other members of the Quartz family, Citrine is great to use for giving yourself an energy boost. Doing so regularly has many wonderful "side effects."

First, Citrine instantly balances all chakras. I like to place a piece on each of my seven main chakra centers for an amazing overall balancing.

Citrine's second quality should get your attention: its frequency resonates with material abundance, or money. Using this stone can actually increase your bank balance.

Here's how: there is an energetic flow in the universe that is conducive to cash flow, and its frequency is strikingly similar to that of Citrine.

Citrine is a burned down form of Amethyst.

Therefore, when we place Citrine in our auric field, we begin to vibrate or resonate to that frequency, thereby attracting wealth to ourselves. This quality has given Citrine the moniker "the merchant's stone," because it is such an effective tool to use in the cash drawer of any retail shop.

As I mentioned earlier, I work at a lot of tradeshows and I never go out my front door without my Citrine in my cash pouch. It is a wonderful tool!

At the beginning of the book, I mentioned the steady client who needed a particular stone run over his auric field in order to assist him in dealing with abundance issues. Citrine was the stone I used.

It is an extremely powerful abundance stone to keep around.

Sixteen
Kyanite

Chakra: *Throat*
Chemical Composition: *Aluminum Silicate*
Found in: *Switzerland, Italy, Austria, France, Brazil*

Kyanite is another one of my favorite stones. I realize I say that a lot, and I suppose it is because I believe that stones come into our lives at different times to heal us, depending on the area of our bodies or lives that needs work at the time.

Each stone we choose can play a special part in our lives facilitating changes we are seeking. Its potential to help you on your spiritual path and self-discovery process is unlimited. It has been a tremendous help to me in my journey. It comes in elongated shards of blue and white and is one of the only other stones I know of, besides Citrine, that never needs cleansing. It is, therefore, a great one to use to balance the chakras.

Kyanite is a stone of the unconscious mind. It helps us to dream and to access other realms and dimensions. It can also facilitate channeling, which is why I was first attracted to it. Because it can also dispel insomnia, I decided to start sleeping with Kyanite blades under my head, neck and back.

Over time, I began to notice outstanding results. At first, I dreamed a lot, which I originally thought was simply a by-product of sleeping better.

The dreams themselves were often strange, disturbing, and incredibly detailed, and I found I remembered them more often upon wakening. As time passed, I continued to dream more frequently, but the dreams began to seem "cleaner," as if I had cleared some of the clutter I had been storing in my mind.

I like to tell people that your unconscious mind is like a huge garage that you continuously pile loads of stuff into. After a while, you may consider doing "spring cleaning" and clearing all of that out.

I believe Kyanite is spring cleaning for the mind: using it made me feel as if I had taken a big

Top: Stunning Blue Kyanite specimen and blades.
Bottom: Delicate Black Kyanite

broom and swept the cobwebs out of my mind. Since I began using it, I find that my dreams are clear communication from my higher self and that I can remember and follow the directions I've received easily upon awakening.

Recently I was teaching my crystal healing class at a local metaphysical shop and I always pass around each stone I talk about so the group can hold it and experience it firsthand.

One of my students was adamant about the Kyanite and said that she refused to hold it because it makes her sick!

I have heard of strong reactions such as this to elements of the earth, and as a regression therapist, I am inclined to believe this woman may have some karmic ties to the stone.

To this date, I have yet to confirm or deny this, however, I remember taking a class once where we were asked to resolve karma with each of the four elements: earth, air, fire and water. I found that I had unresolved karma with water, and have since discovered it has ties back to the destruction of Atlantis.

Kyanite is very fragile. I never put mine outside unless I am sure I can get to it in a reasonable amount of time. Although it does not *need* to be cleaned, I feel all of my stones want to return to the mother from time to time, so I put them out anyway. Just use caution with Kyanite and never put it out in the rain.

Another even more delicate version of Kyanite is black and fans out more. In my experience, it works the same as the blue version, but keeps the subject more grounded to Earth while doing so. It is so delicate, though, that you cannot sleep on it, so I keep in next to my headboard.

Kyanite also comes in green, the primary color of healing support and the heart. If you need more healing energies of this type, perhaps green would work best for you.

Seventeen
Sodalite

Chakra: *Throat*
Chemical Composition: *Chloric Sodium Aluminum Silicate*
Found in: *Montana, Brazil, India, Canada, Colorado*

      I first discovered Sodalite thanks to a friend who suggested it may help me with my hypoglycemic tendencies. I would get very hungry throughout the day and if I did not eat a snack or something with sugar in it right away, I would "crash and burn" energetically. Additionally—though it was never confirmed by a medical doctor—my chiropractor suggested I may have a slight thyroid imbalance.

Sodalite is excellent for anything to do with thyroid or glandular conditions. It works to balance the lymph system and restore normalcy to the body. Since using it, I no longer feel the hypoglycemic symptoms, which is a relief.

Sodalite is very soothing to the touch, and its deep blue color makes it an excellent communication stone for work on the throat chakra.

When I began teaching my basic gems class and needed an inexpensive, easily accessible blue stone to work with the throat, Sodalite was the one I chose. My students like it because of its beauty. It has intricate white streaks, composed primarily of Calcite, throughout.

Sodalite is a gentle stone. Some of the stones I discuss later cause more of a shock to the system as they heal and remove blockages, but Sodalite seems to gently and compassionately bring the body into balance and harmony.

I have my own personal stones I like to use and once when teaching a class I accidentally picked up my long time piece of Sodalite by accident and took it to the class.

Opposite page: Rough (top) and polished Sodalite

It was a *stunning* small piece, so of course, somebody wanted to buy it.

As I looked to see which piece the student had picked up, I immediately realized what I had done.

When she took it in her hand after paying for it, the stone cracked into several pieces instantaneously! I had never seen anything like it! It was amazing!

Apparently I had offended the little stone and it decided it was not going home with anyone else! The woman picked out another one, and that was the last time I ever let that happen!

Another great story involved a client who used the tranquil energies of Sodalite to help her son.

The client said her five-year-old son was having trouble in school and had been diagnosed with minor speech delays.

She decided to try placing a piece of Sodalite in his pillowcase to see what would happen. Within a relatively short period of time (three weeks) she noticed a subtle, yet noticeable improvement in his condition.

Her son has a very sweet and gentle spirit, so it was not surprising to me that he resonated with the calming frequencies of Sodalite.

Eighteen

Jasper

Chakra: *Sacral*
Chemical Composition: *Silicon Dioxide*
Found in: *Michigan, California, Arkansas, Madagascar*

The name "Jasper" comes from a Greek word that means "spotted stone." All Jaspers are from the Chalcedony family and there are many types of the stone found in the world today. The two types of Jasper I most enjoy using and would like to share with you here are Red Jasper and Orbitcular Jasper.

Red Jasper

When I was looking for stones for my class,

I wanted to find a readily available stone that would work with the second chakra. I found Red Jasper to be an excellent candidate. It is similar to Sodalite in that it has a gentle nature and peacefully brings balance to the body.

Red Jasper's actual color is dark reddish orange, which resonates best with the second, or sacral chakra. All forms of Jasper seem to have a soothing effect on the digestive process and the stomach, and Red Jasper is no exception to that rule. Red Jasper is often spotted and contains inclusions and streaks, but I prefer to work with the solid red version of the stone in healing.

I later began to explore other uses of this stone. I had heard that Red Jasper could be used to help people with insomnia and dream recall. I decided to try it, and slept in a bed full of Red Jasper for a week to see what happened.

Sure enough, it did seem to bring up more dreams I could easily remember the next morning. The feeling upon awakening, though, was different than when I used the Kyanite. It was a gentler, more natural feeling and seemed to have Native American energies. Indeed, Red Jasper is an excellent stone to meditate on when attempting to contact your animal spirit guides.

The only problem I had with the Red Jasper

came from lying on the polished, tumbled stones. During the night I kept feeling like something hurt and I would wake up and find myself lying on a rock! Kyanite's flat blades are certainly gentler in that respect.

I recommend experimenting with both to see what you discover the differences to be.

Orbitcular Jasper

Orbitcular Jasper is the other type of Jasper I really love. It is one of the most interesting stones I have ever seen. It comes from Madagascar, an island of off the coast of Africa. Each stone is full of beautiful color and intricate design: they can be burnt orange, bright yellow, green, white, or any combination of those colors. Each piece is so unique it is like artwork.

As with the other Jaspers, I have meditated with the orbitcular version to ease stomach tension. The round circles found in the stone remind me of our intestines and digestive system and the stone works well to put them at ease and to create harmony within the body in this area. It is nature giving us her best in the form of physical beauty and is among my clients' favorites of the gemstones in my collection.

Nineteen
Carnelian

Chakra: *Sacral*
Chemical Composition: *Silicon Dioxide*
Found in: *Brazil, India, Uruguay*

Perhaps a better, yet more intense, choice to use for opening the second chakra is called Carnelian. It is an excellent protective stone to be used against psychic attack and is the carrier of the orange color ray.

When I mention psychic attack in my classes I am amazed to see a great number of people do not know what I am talking about.

We have mentioned the phenomena of thoughts as "things" that take a definite shape and space in our universe.

When people think about you, it creates a thoughtform.

Hopefully, the thoughts others think about us are positive, yet unfortunately, this is not always the case.

When negative thoughts are willfully sent to another person, particularly one who is sensitive to energy, this can be viewed as a form of psychic attack.

Carnelian is excellent for creating a protective shield against negativity.

It can also aid those with digestive troubles. A client of mine read in *The Secret Language of Birthdays* that Carnelian was especially beneficial to those born under the sign of Virgo (which she was).

Since Virgo rules the intestines, people born under that sign are prone to indigestion and all manner of digestive distress, and my Virgo client was no exception: she jokingly referred to Tums as "after dinner mints."

According to the book, Carnelian would help Virgo natives suffering from stomach troubles.

Opposite page: the beautiful Carnelian

Figuring she had nothing to lose but a few cents, my client tried it out. She is pleased to report that one stone achieved what countless bottles of Tums couldn't: she now rarely suffers from indigestion.

More interestingly, she has significantly lightened not one, but two stones. This is probably due to the fact that she is absorbing some of the life force from the stone.

She cleans them regularly and continues to use them for healing support.

Twenty
Obsidian

Chakra: *Root*
Chemical Composition: *Volcanic Rock*
Found in: *Mexico, Wyoming, Hungary, Japan*

Although Obsidian is actually volcanic glass, it is one of the many minerals, because of its beauty, to transcend the rock category. It is now considered to be a semiprecious gemstone.

Depending on where it is found, Obsidian occurs in many spectacular forms. My favorite is Snowflake Obsidian, a beautiful black stone with white spots resembling snowflakes. It is sometimes hard to find this form.

Rainbow Obsidian looks black at first

glance, but when you hold it to the light you can see prisms that shine like rainbows.

Apache Tears are another form of Obsidian. I have some that my grandmother collected near a volcano in New Mexico. Native Americans called them Apache Tears because as ash spews out of a volcano, it drops like rain to the ground and forms small balls of matter that actually resemble hardened teardrops. They are really interesting and special when you can find them.

Apache Tears from a volcano in New Mexico
Opposite Page: Rainbow Obsidian (top) and Snowflake

Much of the Obsidian we see in jewelry is the gorgeous deep black variety. People like to wear Obsidian, like many stones we have already discussed, because of the grounding and extreme protection the stone gives the wearer. Many cultures use it in protective amulets.

Twenty-One
Smoky Quartz

Chakra: *Root*
Chemical Composition: *Silicon Dioxide*
Found in: *Brazil, Madagascar, Russia, Switzerland, Scotland*

Another of the most protective of all healing gemstones is Smoky Quartz. You may have heard Smoky Quartz referred to as Smoky Topaz; however, gemologists no longer use this term.

In Part 3 of the book I have an exercise in which you will meditate with a piece of Smoky Quartz and imagine you are inside the stone because it is such a great protector. I still love using

Smoky Quartz anytime I need to feel grounded.

This gem, like Hematite and Garnet, works to keep the energies of others from harming you, and just as we have seen with both of those stones, it too must be cleansed regularly.

I think of stones as stimulants or depressants. Though Quartz is a stimulant, the smoky version, because of its darker color, allows us to ground, and therefore promotes rest. It is the only member of the Quartz family I recommend using at night. All of the others tend to keep people awake.

Here's one of my favorite stories about Smoky Quartz. Some time ago, I visited my friend who owns the African Gallery in Denver, where I bought the Hematite necklace. I quickly noticed numerous boxes of stones laying on the floor of his office.

I immediately began rummaging through them and was shocked to find several stunning pieces of Smoky Quartz just sitting there as if they were scrap. Several were gemgrade quality and were absolutely gorgeous.

Opposite: Top: gem grade Smoky point from South Africa Bottom: Two South African points with Aegerine inclusions imbedded in the stone.

"Do you realize what these are?" I asked excitedly.

Of course, he had no clue. He just thought they were junk compared with his Tanzanites and Emeralds. Needless to say, I "rescued" the Smoky Quartz and took the stones back to Texas. They were quickly "adopted" by people who really appreciated them.

I think of myself as a pet rock adoption agency. My job is to not fall too much in love with the stones and to help them find homes elsewhere with the people who were meant to have them.

Twenty-Two
Aegerine

Chakra: *Root*
Chemical Composition: *Sodium Iron Silicate*
Found in: *Arkansas, Montana, USSR, Canada*

Also in the "junk pile" at the African art gallery were some stunning pieces of Aegerine. As you saw in the last chapter, some Smoky Quartz crystals occur with Aegerine blades protruding from them, which makes them really interesting.

Aegerine comes in blades, similar to Kyanite. Its chemical composition produces a dark, nearly black color and can be quite grounding.

I had learned the stone builds a strong immune system. The friend I was staying with during this particular trip to Denver with was ill with a fever and bronchitis symptoms. I did not want to catch whatever he had, so I began meditating with the Aegerine blades. I am pleased to say that I feel it warded off the illness altogether.

This is yet another example of the fact that "one man's junk is another man's treasure," although now that my gallery owner friend knows what Aegerine can do, he is using it himself!

Aegerine blades from South Africa

Twenty-Three
Aventurine

Chakra: *Heart*
Chemical Composition: *Silicon Dioxide*
Found in: *Brazil, India Austria, Russia, Africa*

Have you ever lay down in bed at night and realized you were in intense pain because you had worked yourself to the point of absolute exhaustion?

That's how I first discovered the healing powers of Aventurine. I had received a very special piece of the stone from my Native American friend. I decided to start lying on it at night to dispel my aches and pains. Within a couple of minutes of doing so, I would feel a thousand times better!

A wonderful "side effect" of that practice, which I did not realize at the time, is that Aventurine is one of those special stones that attracts wealth and abundance.

I soon began noticing that my business was picking up more than usual. I eventually pieced together that the increase may be linked to my continual use of the Aventurine. Now, I never go to a show without that stone in my purse or cash pouch. It is an essential part of my standard "equipment" that I do not leave home without.

Some of my clients have reported similar results after using the stone. One received a settlement within two weeks of meditating with Aventurine and Citrine. Another received a pay raise at work. Is it "luck" or is this stone actually working? That doesn't seem to matter as long as the results are there!

Green and Yellow Aventurine

Twenty-Four
Agate

Chakra: *Throat, Root, Sacral*
Chemical Composition: *Silicon Dioxide (Chalcedony family)*
Found in: *Uruguay, India, Brazil*

There are many types of Agate in the world and I would like to discuss two of my favorites here: Blue Lace Agate and Moss Agate.

Blue Lace Agate

I first used Blue Lace Agate early in my journey with the healing gemstones. Like most

Agate, this stone features beautiful circular bands running throughout. Its light blue color means it helps us with everything having to do with communicating our truth and with opening the throat chakra. It is also particularly helpful with balancing the immune system.

Moss Agate

I also enjoy Moss Agate because it is so unique. Unlike most Agate, this stone is not banded at all, but is white with amazing dark green dendrite fernlike inclusions. It also occurs in dark green with brown fernlike inclusions.

Moss Agate helps us learn to communicate with the plant kingdom and can also attract abundance, more in the realm of food and natural abundance than that of material abundance. When our table is set and we have all we want to eat, that creates a feeling both of simple abundance and of comfort in the knowledge that our basic needs are met easily and effortlessly. Moss Agate can help create that feeling.

Opposite page: Blue Lace Agate (top), an unusual Agate specimen (center), Moss Agate (bottom).

The stone can also be a tool for making rain and cloud busting, and for averting inclement weather. My brother, like many people, has an obsession with weather. He swears Moss Agate is the stone that causes our rainstorms and keeps us safe from natural disasters.

Agate in general is very soothing and is so beautiful because it comes in such a wide variety of colors and designs depending on where they are found. They are also one of the most common types of stones around.

Many of the banded looking turquoise blue or hot pink dyed slabs found in souvenir shops are made of Agate.

Twenty-Five
Bloodstone

Chakra: *Root, Sacral*
Chemical Composition: *Silicon Dioxide*
Found in: *India, Australia, Brazil, China, United States*

The Bloodstone is another member of the Chalcedony family. It is said that this amazing stone was found in the breastplate of the high priests in ancient times. Bloodstone is usually dull, dark green to yellow/gold in color, and often has red spots throughout. It is thought that the red spots found in the stone represent the blood of Christ, and that perhaps this was the stone placed under Him during His crucifixion. Regardless of whether this is the case, the Bloodstone could easily be associated with Christ, simply because it is always willing to sacrifice itself in order to help us heal.

My first book, *Origins of Huna: Secret Behind the Secret Science,* described some of the healing practices of the ancient Hawaiians and the term they used for the lifeforce is *mana.* The ancient Hawaiians believed every living thing mother earth gave us possessed special healing powers. Should you happen to get a piece of Bloodstone that includes the red spots to aid you on your own healing journey, the spots will likely disappear over time as you meditate with the stone because you will literally take on the lifeforce of the stone itself.

Bloodstone is also one of the most amazing stones available for raising the *kundalini* (serpent energy), which, according to Eastern doctrine, is located at the base of our spine. The stone is also most effective for balancing all of the chakras.

Spiritually, Bloodstone is all about love, and cleansing and healing the heart emotionally. Medicinally, it aids with blood circulation and with cleans-

Opposite: the translucent white part of this Bloodstone shows an example of the red being absorbed by the body.

ing impurities from the blood. It can also help those suffering from any sort of heart problem.

Of all the stones I discuss in this book I have seen the most amazing healing results with the Bloodstone.

I had a client who was very ill with a strange lung problem that, as far as I know, remains undiagnosed. Since circulation is also a function of the lungs, I recommended he use the Bloodstone for healing support.

He took it home and called me the next day to say he left his cell phone in my office and that he needed to meet me somewhere to pick it up. He also said he had something astonishing to show me.

When we met, he took the Bloodstone he had gotten only the day before out of his pocket. I was shocked as I looked at it and saw that his body had not only absorbed the red from the stone, it had absorbed the rest of the color from it as well. It now looked like a clear shell, and I could see the stone had been almost eaten away from the inside.

If I had any doubt that this stuff works, I was a true believer after seeing that with my own eyes! It was unreal!

Twenty-Six
Garnet

Chakra: *Root*
Chemical Composition: *Aluminum Silicate*
Found in: *Madagascar, Sri Lanka, South Africa, Brazil, China, United States*

In ancient times, the Garnet was often confused with the Ruby. It was not until fairly recently, when stones' chemical compositions could be determined, that it was noted that the group of stones known as Garnet are comprised of aluminum silicate. Other minerals occurring in individual stones give each Garnet a unique composition.

I love Garnet jewelry. It conveys a peaceful, grounding feeling that is hard to describe.

Garnet is another stone of love and commitment in addition, it is an extremely powerful protector.

Earlier in the book I spoke about psychic attack, when someone or something willfully sends negative thoughtforms to you to wreak havoc on your very existence.

Once on vacation, I stayed at the Oxford Hotel in the historic district of Lower Downtown Denver. Years ago, I served as membership director for the district, so when I can, I enjoy staying in the old hotel. Built in the late 1800's, it is the oldest hotel in Denver.

Everyone in Denver knows this place is haunted, although if you ask the staff there, they won't admit it openly, lest the tourists should be scared away.

During this particular visit to The Oxford, I was constantly met in the hallway by a "presence" with an enormous amount of energy. Not necessarily negative, but extremely powerful.

A few days into my stay, after running into the energy in the hall again, I went into my room and shut the door.

I was wearing an antique Garnet necklace,

Opposite: The antique Garnet necklace after repair.

still on its original string, at the time. I looked at myself in the mirror and could not believe what I saw. The string appeared to smoke as if it were on fire and the necklace fell to the floor.

Upon further reflection, I put two and two together. The Garnet reminded me of Hematite at that moment, because I later learned that Garnet is another great stone for deflecting negative or powerful energies and, as such, it needs to be cleansed frequently. In my case, the stone had apparently taken in all it could, and could do nothing else but fall to the ground.

Twenty-Seven
Moonstone

Chakra: *Third Eye*
Chemical Composition: *Potassium Aluminum Silicate*
Found in: *Brazil, Madagascar, India, U.S.*

Long before I ever got into crystal and gemstone healing, and ever since I can remember, I have always loved to wear Moonstone jewelry.

In the Tarot, the Moon card is symbolic of deep thinking and that which is hidden below the surface. Moonstone symbolizes the feminine aspect of consciousness. Because it resonates with the Moon itself, Moonstone is also a great tool for helping with insomnia and the dream state. In addition, it can be used as a protective amulet while traveling, which may explain why I love it so much; I always seem to be going somewhere!

A few years ago I was in Luxor, Egypt, home of the Valley of the Kings (the location of the tombs of the Egyptian Pharaohs). My tour guide took me to a jewelry shop run by a friend of his.

I had selected some bracelets and was in line to pay when my head jerked suddenly to one side. I found myself staring at a Moonstone ring that I had not previously noticed. Although the stone in it was not as high-grade as the one in the Moonstone ring I had left in the States, it was attractive and I liked the shape, so I decided to buy it.

In his book *Reunions*, Dr. Raymond Moody details the ancient art of scrying into a crystal ball to see future events or people who have passed into spirit.

During a scrying class I once took at a metaphysical shop, we were asked to bring a crystal. We put scarves over our heads to cut down on the light, turned out the lights, and stared into the crystal in hopes of seeing a vision.

It took quite a while to get to the point where I could see anything and there was a definite process to doing so. I ended up seeing a dreamlike vision of a mountain valley with a river running

Two different types of Moonstone and my Egyptian ring.

through it. It seemed to be a symbolic message from my unconscious mind.

I tell you this because when I bought this mysterious Moonstone ring, I soon noticed that when I would look down into the stone it seemed, with no warning, to light up with a bluish color as if someone were shining a light behind it.

I also noticed I could see the faces of many diverse kinds of people blowing by as if they were being carried by the wind. I saw ladies with big fluffy hats from the old west, hardened cowboy-looking people, Indian chiefs, African people, and children. They seemed to be from all walks of life.

Was there some sort of portal to the other side in this stone, I wondered? I thought I might be insane when it first started happening (which seems to be something I check into from time to time in my life) so I decided to get another opinion.

I took the ring to my dad and asked him to wear it for several hours while I ran an errand. When I returned, I asked him if he saw anything, and he admitted that he did!

After some time, the appearances stopped. I have no way of knowing whether this is a quality of Moonstones in general, but I am inclined to think this particular stone was special, because it came from such a spiritually powerful part of the world.

Twenty-Eight
Tektite

Chakra: *Root*
Chemical Composition: *Volcanic Rock*
Found in: *Czechoslovakia, Tibet, worldwide*

Moldavite

Among the most interesting classes of stones in the world are the Tektites which are composed of meteors that have fallen to earth. Of particular interest to me is the unique Moldavite, supposedly the only stone of true extraterrestrial origin. It is only found in one spot in Czechoslovakia. Since it is extremely rare, Moldavite is sold by the gram.

Geologists site that Moldavite is composed of silicon dioxide formed by the earth being hit by a meteorite, thus the extraterrestrial origins theory. It comes in an unusual translucent green color ranging from light to dark.

While Tektites in general are powerful protective stones that stimulate the root chakra, Moldavite is a unique activator of the third eye and crown.

Moldavite links us to our extraterrestrial brothers and sisters in space and enables communication between us.

I first heard of Moldavite when I bought a few pieces at the Tucson Gem and Mineral Show. Although I nearly choked at the price, I found it to be a worthy investment later on, because of the stone's high frequency and its amazing healing capacity.

The best way I know to describe Moldavite's effects on the body is to compare it to something you've probably experienced: chocolate

Opposite: Top: An example of the translucent Moldavite Bottom: Tibetan Tektite I use with my regression clients.

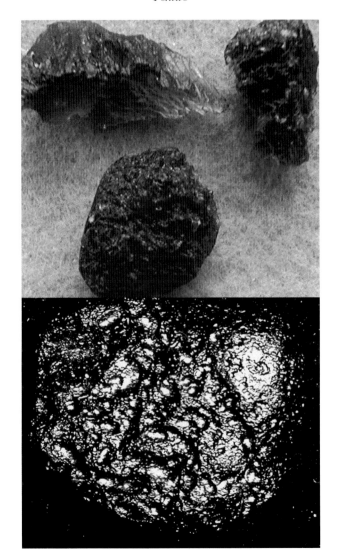

covered espresso beans. Though the really good ones are addictive, too many will "send you into orbit!"

Meditating with Moldavite feels as if you have eaten a few espresso beans and are just beginning to get that amazing surge of energy. The good news is that unlike the coffee beans-which eventually cause you to crash and burn-Moldavite wears off gradually, leaving you in much better shape than before.

I had sold all but one piece of my first batch of Moldavite when I decided to sell my personal piece because a client wanted it. When I tried to reach for it, though, it seemed to jump from my hands and went under a chair! Apparently, my brethren in space were not too thrilled with my attempt to thwart our lines of communication!

Tibetan Tektite

A friend in the gem business asked me to test a piece of Tibetan Tektite. It is different from the Moldavite because it is heavy and black and closely resembles a standard volcanic rock.

I had been told that Tektites are powerful aids in the recall of past lives. Since I was doing a great deal of work in that area at the time, I decided to give it to clients to hold during their past-life regression sessions.

The results were phenomenal. One client practically regressed to scores of different lifetimes spontaneously. I have never seen that before, nor have I since.

Although I do not like to dwell too much on each life in my sessions, I believed my client was visiting each lifetime a bit too briefly in this regression. I felt there was not enough time to examine the individual lives to recognize prevailing patterns and to heal past wounds. The next time my client came in, I did not use the stone so the process could be more thorough.

I must say, though, that the Tektite ultimately made it easier to tap into my client's past lives in the second session and to clear things up, because it opened the door to so many lives during the initial session. I concluded, therefore, that Tektite is a useful tool to employ in past-life regression when I feel guided to do so.

Twenty-Nine
Infinite

Chakra: *Heart, overall healer*
Chemical Composition: *Magnesium Silicate*
Found in: *South Africa*

Infinite is a fairly new stone. It looks like a simple greenish river rock and probably wouldn't attract your attention if you had no idea how wonderful it is.

I cannot share with certainty Infinite's chemical composition because it is not specifically addressed in any gemology books, nor could I find it in the wonderful, comprehensive *Love is in the Earth: A Kaleidoscope of Crystals*, by A. Melody. It is supposedly a form of Serpentine, so I have included that as the composition of the stone.

Infinite seems to appear primarily in green with occasional banding, and a white matrix that appears so similar to that found in Sodalite that I am inclined to think the matrix must be calcite.

It makes sense to me that Infinite contains calcium somewhere, because it is the best stone I have ever encountered for treating bone disorders

Surprisingly, Infinite looks like a simple river rock!

and aches and pains stemming from diseases such as arthritis. It is the best stone I have ever seen for providing relief from extreme pain.

I once used Infinite on my mom to alleviate a horrible ache in her shoulder. She literally taped some on each side of her sore shoulder; within hours the pain was almost gone.

Whenever I happen to have Infinite on hand in a class, any experienced healers in the group snap it up because it is not always readily available. One of my healer friends bought some to help her father, who was suffering from cancer. Apparently, it was the best thing she had ever found to help ease his pain naturally.

Infinite is a soothing stone that conveys a nurturing feeling to the user as it gently removes pain and discomfort.

I highly recommend adding Infinite to your "metaphysical first aid kit." You never know when it will come in handy!

Thirty
Emerald

Chakra: *Heart*
Chemical Composition: *Aluminum Beryllium Silicate*
Found in: *Africa, South America, India*

Emerald in its natural form is one of the most powerful healers on our planet. It is the carrier of the green color ray, so it is excellent for the activation of the heart chakra. Many of the Emeralds sold in American jewelry stores are created in laboratories. The lab-created gems lack the healing properties of the natural stones.

Like all of the green stones, Emerald provides overall healing support, particularly for healing heart problems. Emerald elixirs can aid in this way.

One client had recently been diagnosed with congestive heart failure. He came to me for energy work and I suggested a piece of Emerald.

After using the stone everyday for a week, his chest pains subsided completely, never to return again. Emeralds also help circulation, which the client reported had also improved.

The medical doctor who originally diagnosed him has since said the congestion has subsided.

Miracles such as this are possible in all our lives if we are open to them.

Most of us are not used to seeing low grade tumbled Emeralds. They look quite different from the laboratory creations found in most jewelry.

Thirty-One
Celestite

Chakra: *Throat*
Chemical Composition: *Strontium Sulfate*
Found in: *Madagascar*

     Celestite is a stunning, light blue crystal stone and is one of the many light blue varieties of stones that promote universal love and communication from the heart.

     A friend introduced me to Celestite when she suggested I purchase a stone as a birthday gift for my mother. In *Love is in the Earth,* Melody agrees that Celestite is a great gift for those you love and respect.

I now use this stone quite a bit in healing sessions. Once I discovered its power, I began using it to cleanse the subtle energy bodies of the client, primarily because of its powerful vibration of pure love.

Celestite helps us develop self-love at the spiritual causal plane so we may bring that feeling of self-acceptance down to our conscious existence.

Celestite makes a beautiful gift!

Thirty-Two
Apatite

Chakra: *Throat, Solar Plexus*
Chemical Composition: *Calcium Fluoride*
Found in: *Austria, Maine, Canada, USSR, Sweden, South Africa, Mexico*

As the name suggests, this stone is used to suppress the appetite, and can therefore be an instrumental tool in weight-loss programs.

I have also found it brings a calm, peaceful feeling of balance to my system. I lay it on my stomach to calm me down when I feel stressed-definitely a healthier practice than reaching for the chocolate!

Clients have reported feelings of appetite suppression when using the stone.

Top: Apatite in the rough

Thirty-Three
Herkimer Diamond

Chakra: *Crown*
Chemical Composition: *Carbon*
Found in: *Herkimer, NY*

      Herkimer Diamonds are quite the phenom-
enon of the New Age. They look like clear Quartz,
but it is the energetic charge they possess that
makes them truly remarkable. As the name suggests, they come from one particular spot in

Herkimer, New York.

A client of mine was instantly drawn to a particular piece of Herkimer, but when she picked it up, it gave her a charge so powerful it actually hurt her arm at first. After holding the stone for a couple of minutes, however, the pain subsided and changed to an extreme energetic charge. She wasn't sure if she should take it because of her initial reaction to it, but I encouraged her to go ahead: she was attracted to it for some reason, and perhaps it was healing her in unimaginable ways. Now, it has become one of her favorites in her collection of stones.

There is a theory in New Age circles that the human DNA is shifting and recoding itself as the

Herkimer Diamonds

population reaches consistently higher levels of awareness. Due to its high potency, the Herkimer Diamond is a stone said to facilitate this process.

Though Herkimer Diamonds can be hard to find, I recommend trying them. They give me an enormous surge of energy in meditation and the mental clarity to finish projects. They seem to reconnect neurotransmitters in the brain and to open new pathways for consciousness to occur. I can actually feel my brain tingle when I use them. Perhaps this is the DNA reconnecting.

Thirty-Four
Lepidolite

Chakra: *Third Eye*
Chemical Composition: *Hydrous Potassium Lithium Aluminum Silicate*
Found in: *Australia, California, New Mexico, USSR, Canada, Brazil, Sweden*

Another great stone to use for dream recall is Lepidolite. It is an interesting, delicate lavender-colored granular stone that can assist us in reaching higher planes of consciousness.

I have used it at night to dispel insomnia and to assist my dreams. Its frequency "buzz" is higher than that of Kyanite, and its effect on the psyche feels a bit more abrupt.

My brother has used Lepidolite quite extensively and it is his favorite stone. He says it assists him on his far-out astral trips and that it makes the experiences easier to bring into consciousness on this plane, because the Lepidolite seems to heighten the vividness of the astral experience.

Because of its porous nature, Lepidolite is extremely delicate. Like Kyanite, it does not need to be cleansed after use, yet I do enjoy putting it outside, usually in moonlight, to give it an extra charge. Use care not to put it outside during inclement weather; the stone is so fragile it will suffer damage and possibly disintegrate.

Lepidolite stones are extremely delicate and can be found polished (left) or in an unusual mica.

Thirty-Five
Mookite/

Australian Tiger Iron

Chakra: *Root*
Chemical Composition: *Silicon Dioxide with Iron Oxide*
Found in: *Australia, New Zealand*

While in Tucson, I found an amazing new stone called Mookite, which gave me the chills when I picked it up and held it. It seemed to wake up a part of me that had been asleep, perhaps stirring feelings from a past life. I'm not the only one who is profoundly affected by Mookite: I do not even own any at this time because people snap it up as fast as I can get it.

Mookite appears to have some features of standard Red Jasper and often appears with yellow in it, the consistency of that found in Tiger's Eye. It can also have white and black streaks in it. I am inclined to think it is probably nothing more than a simple Jasper, or a member of the Chalcedony species.

It should not really be that remarkable, yet people are literally freaked out by it. What makes it so distinctive is its energy.

Earlier in the book, when I told the story about the crucifix from Jerusalem, I talked about the power of objects as they relate to their place of origin. Similarly, I believe stones can affect us depending on what part of the world they are from.

I think that is why Mookite is so powerful. It takes the user to other dimensions and allows us to tap into the collective consciousness of the indigenous peoples of the Australian/New Zealand area of the world for healing. It taps into Aboriginal consciousness, which can be quite helpful to us in our quest for knowledge of healing.

The Aborigines are fascinating people

because they are able to communicate telepathically and can actually share consciousness with each other. What one person sees may be transmitted to his tribe via a shared vision.

Perhaps there is another reason for my strong attraction to the stone. I recently had my astrocartography chart erected. Astrocartography is a process in which an astrologer prints out your birth chart, then lays it on a map of the world to show how the planets were aligned the day you were born. Planetary alignment over specific regions can have an effect on how you like or dislike particular areas of the world. When I had my chart done, I was told I could be blissfully happy if I ever moved to or visited a small town on the south island of New Zealand.

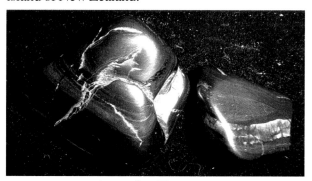

Australian Tiger Iron

I may love Mookite so much because astrologically, I am aligned with that part of the world. Perhaps others who are drawn to it may have connections to that area, or may have lived there in a previous lifetime.

I also recently picked up some Australian Tiger Iron, which is another stone that seems common, yet has those special regional energies attached to it. The gemological term for this stone is Tiger's Eye Matrix. Australian Tiger Iron occurs when a Tiger's Eye-like substance (member of the quartz family consisting of silicon dioxide) is mixed in with iron oxide.

People seem to be drawn to it for the same reasons they are attracted to Mookite. Tiger Iron is an extremely grounding stone due to its iron content and has great energy.

If there is a particular part of the world you are attracted to, I recommend buying a stone from that region to see what happens.

Thirty-Six
Boji Stones

Chakra: *Hands - used for balancing*
Chemical Composition: *unknown*
Found in: *Kansas*

Of all the rocks, gems and minerals I have encountered, the Bojis seem the most like living creatures.

They come only from one place in Kansas and usually come in pairs-one male and one female. I have also worked with a single-stone variety that has a strange, shiny top, but I like the pairs best because the yin/yang energy of the two together is extremely powerful.

I purchased a couple of sets of Bojis that I planned to sell at an upcoming show. One morning just before dawn, I "heard" the smallest pair call to me from the hall. They wanted me to come and get them and when I did, I fell head over heels in love with them.

Bojis remind me most of those pet rocks from the 1970's. They are really cute little characters. Each set, and individual stone within the set, has its own unique personality.

There is male and female energy within each of us, and I use Bojis to balance my yin/yang energy. Because the stones are male and female, I use a polarity theory to allow their energies to balance my system. Energetically, the right hand and side of a person is the male side; the left is the female.

A good practice for all of us is to meditate on balancing the male/female energies within us. We can do this by simply asking our higher self to do it, or we may use Boji Stones to facilitate the process.

I have found putting the "male" stone in the female (left) hand and the "female" stone in the male (right) hand is the best way to use the pair. Lie still and you will begin to feel the balancing occur. The shift can be quite dramatic.

Since it worked so well in meditation, I decided I should carry the stones in my pocket, the male in my left pocket and female in my right, for an entire day. After several hours I checked in with my Bojis, and I intuitively felt they were very unhappy. They are like a couple and become discombobulated and upset when they are separated from the one they love.

From then on, I have always been very conscious to lay them next to each other after each use and to carry them in the same pocket while transporting them.

Clients who have used them are also "in love" with the little Bojis. They are truly remarkable.

Male (left) and female (right) Boji Stones.

Thirty-Seven
Sugilite/ Manganese

Chakra: *Root, Third Eye*
Chemical Composition: *Potassium Sodium Ferric Magnesium Aluminum Lithium Silicate*
Found in: *Brazil, Africa*

Before I ever even knew of the powers of Sugilite alone, I acquired a fabulous piece of Sugilite/Manganese that quickly became one of my favorite stones of all of those in my collection, and is to this day.

Sugilite is a fairly new violet-colored stone

(previously known as Sogdianite in the gem world) that is extremely powerful in assisting us with accessing the psychic realm and with opening the third eye. Manganese is a form of iron oxide that usually occurs in the ocean floor. The addition of this substance to the Sugilite brings grounding and centeredness to the task of opening the third eye.

My guides directed me to use this stone on my third eye at night before going to sleep. It is very powerful and peaceful at the same time. My intuition has become much clearer since using it and my precognitive visions of the future have not only increased, but have become stunningly accurate as a result of using the Sugilite.

My favorite piece of Sugilite/Manganese!

Thirty-Eight
Selenite

Chakra: *Crown*
Chemical Composition: *Calcium Sulfate*
Found in: *Utah, New Mexico, Texas, Italy, Iran*

Selenite is a wonderful tool for energizing the body. Because it comes in beautiful flat sedimentary pieces, it works wonders on the nervous system by putting your feet on it and allowing energy healing to shoot from your toes to the top of your head.

It does not need cleaning, so it is excellent to use in clearing your crystals and stones when you do not have the luxury of living in a place where you can take your stones outside for clearing.

Lately, I have been using my Selenite quite a bit in meditation.

It seems to open the door to higher dimensions of consciousness and clears all the chakras as well as the etheric and spiritual bodies.

Placed on the crown, it opens your mind to hearing your higher wisdom and guidance.

Selenite opens the crown in a gentle manner, and brings a sense of peace and tranquility to the user.

I think it is beautiful and it is quickly becoming one of my favorite stones to use!

The beautiful Selenite opens you to higher wisdom!

Thirty-Nine
Calcite

Chakra: *Solar Plexus, Sacral*
Chemical Composition: *Calcium Carbonate*
Found in: *Tennessee, Oklahoma, Colorado, Iceland, Germany, Mexico, Italy*

The beautiful crystal featured on the front cover of this book is a piece of Golden Calcite I recently acquired in Hot Springs, Arkansas, from my friend Gary Fleck.

Gary is one of the foremost authorities on Golden Calcite, and crystals in general, and currently has mining rights to one of the largest

Calcite mines in the US.

When I was visiting him in Hot Springs, he mentioned that Golden Calcite is a very important planetary stone at this time. I thought it would be appropriate in this section of the book to ask him to speak directly as to why this stone is emerging at this time. Here is his response:

Calcite crystals in general are rather common on planet Earth. Typical colors are gray, brown to black and various shades of white. Of greater rarity are shades of deep golden color, sometimes referred to as "stellar beam" Golden Calcite. Many examples of these crystals are double terminated and can be quite large in size. The finest Golden Calcite crystals found to date come from a mine near Elmwood, Tennessee.

Crystals from this locality commonly range in size from three to eight inches in length, and are sometimes said to resemble "footballs" in shape. Some exhibit a very rich golden color. Calcite that is either pink or deep green would be considered as very rare.

My inner guidance tells me that "stellar beam" Golden Calcite crystals represent initiation into a higher order of understanding, wisdom, and spiritual presence. There has been a recent surge in demand for these crystals in the past 8 months. Has the energy of these magnificent crystals recently been upgraded, or are we as a planetary whole simply more receptive to the energetic nature of Golden Calcite at this time? If one is drawn to any particular type of crystal, one might ponder "why?" and be open to the possibility of receiving useful information of a personal or universal nature. Of course, we may receive the greatest pleasure and "value" from any crystal by simply enjoying the presence and magic!

Golden Calcite (right) and Red Calcite (left)

Forty
Larimar

Chakra: *Throat, Heart, Third Eye*
Chemical Composition: *Hydrous Sodium Calcium Silicate*
Found in: *Dominican Republic*

I have decided to save the best for last. I could write a whole book about Larimar. Of all the stones I have run across in my lifetime, this one is the most special to me, and I went on quite a journey to find it!

I encountered Larimar at the Tucson Gem and Mineral Show. That in itself is not strange; how

I got there in the first place to "meet" it is. I was in Texas on a Saturday evening when my guides suddenly told me to drive to the show in Tucson the very next morning. Although family and friends thought I was nuts (as I've said, this notion seems to occur to me and my circle from time to time), I quickly packed the car and was on the road by 10:00 the next morning.

I arrived at the showroom with the intention of heading for a booth where a friend was working. Before I reached her, though, I found myself completely mesmerized by a beautiful blue stone I had never seen before.

I talked to Charlie Mark, the operator of the booth and the major player in Larimar distribution, about the stone and why I had never seen it before. It is a relatively new discovery.

A few years ago, Charlie was working in the Diamond and Ruby business and was asked to invest in an experimental mine in the Dominican Republic. That venture produced the extremely rare, one-of-a-kind Larimar, technically referred to

Opposite: Notice the fernlike inclusions in the top and bottom right pieces of Larimar. They appear to be fossilized ferns. The rust color is Hematite. Bottom left is a beautiful pure blue sample.

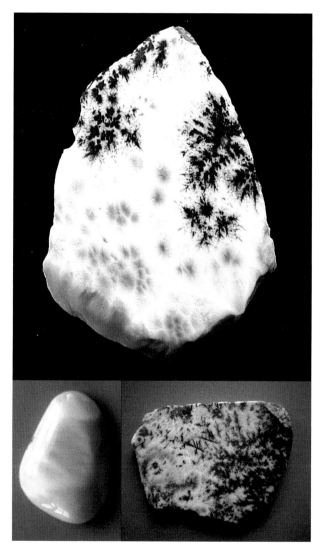

as Blue Pectolyte. It got its trade name from the man who actually first pulled it out of the mine. He named it for his daughter, Larissa, and combined her name with the word "mar" which means sea.

It was soon discovered that this rare gemstone was the one the late, great 20th century "sleeping prophet," Edgar Cayce, wrote about in his writings on Atlantis. When Charlie learned this, he decided to advertise the new find in Vogue magazine. When he showed the ad to his mother, she informed him that the family had actually rented a home from Mr. Cayce before Charlie was born!

Coincidence? I think not! Charlie was obviously destined to make the discovery.

I fell in love with Larimar at first sight. I immediately bought a few pieces and took them back to my hotel room in Tucson. I slept with one of them that night and the vibrational frequency was so high I felt like it would vaporize me into particle matter.

I began having dreams, which continue to this day, of swimming in the ocean and seeing dolphins pass by. Prior to this experience, I had never really thought much about the Atlantis theory, but being introduced to Larimar truly awakened that part of my soul.

On that same night during my dream state,

my guides told me to purchase a large quantity of the stone and to take it back to Dallas with me because it would heal a lot of people.

When I woke the next day, my conscious mind thought this sounded absolutely ludicrous. Surely people in Dallas had Larimar, I thought, but I decided to go ahead and check with Charlie to see. He confirmed that there was not much of it in my area, so I ended up bringing quite a bit back to Texas with me.

I called a few friends who were interested in Atlantis and invited them to a private showing in my home. I was amazed by the word-of-mouth advertising my showing received! Cars lined the streets in front of my home because so many people wanted to come and see the stone.

Larimar has an interesting effect on people. I have found that it opens the heart and the throat so that one may communicate his or her truth with love. (This quality makes it useful for people in the communication professions.) Its ability to promote feelings of self-love is above and beyond the capabilities of any other stone I have encountered in my life.

As a single person, I have often felt I needed to go outside myself to find love. I am sure many of you who are reading this can relate to what

I mean. There was a part of me that felt incomplete unless I was in a relationship. I struggled with this belief for years.

Larimar has helped put the finishing touches on my work in this area. The feelings of self-love and acceptance it promotes and the inner peace it conveys make me feel there is nothing I cannot do. I feel invincible!

I have clients who have felt the same! I took the Larimar out to a small town in East Texas to show to some friends. One man picked up a stone, looked at it, and quickly left the room. He returned about five minutes later and told me that before I got there, he thought all of this stuff he had been hearing about stones was a bunch of garbage. But when he picked up the Larimar, he had such a strong reaction to it he thought he was about to cry like a baby. He had left the room to compose himself. He was now a true believer, and needless to say, he made his first rock purchase that day!

I've heard similar stories from other clients and from friends. Many say the Larimar caused them to have a good, cleansing cry. The tears were not of sorrow, but of joy as their hearts were opened, often for the first time.

Several times I have seen people pick up the Larimar and begin to cry. That is the soul's way of cleansing and healing, and it is a wonderful thing to witness.

Charlie Mark told me that when he takes the stone around to different parts of the world, he has seen people actually begin to shake uncontrollably when they get near the Larimar booth. That reaction is attributable to the large quantities of it in one place, and to the stone's incredibly high vibration.

Melody has said that Larimar vibrates to a master number of 55, yet its frequency seems so much higher to me than that of Turquoise, which is also a 55. It could be, though, that my energetic system has been tuned into Turquoise for so long that it does not affect me the same way as it may affect others. I do know that Larimar's energy is totally different than Turquoise's, though their physical appearance often leads the two stones to be mistaken for one another.

I have another story I feel compelled to share. A client I mentioned earlier-the one with the lung problem who absorbed the life force from the Bloodstone-bought a piece of Larimar the same day. When I saw him the next day, the Larimar had taken on two dark, elongated spots that looked like little lungs.

I cleared it with Reiki and handed it back to

him. It immediately filled up again. I told him to continue using the Larimar to aid his healing and to put it outside often for grounding.

Larimar also taps into dolphin medicine. The dolphin is an amazing creature that is gifted with the incredible ability to communicate on many different levels at once. Larimar has helped me to hear other dimensions of consciousness and to simultaneously stay tuned in to what is going on in this dimension. Medicinally, it is great for headaches or any other blockages of the subtle energy system because of its high vibration.

I mentioned earlier that Larimar is useful in the communications professions, particularly amongst broadcasters. Incredibly, four months after my introduction to Larimar I wound up hosting a weekly metaphysical radio show!

To me, Larimar is the greatest stone on earth. I believe its healing potential is absolutely amazing. I believe it is the very best nature has to offer.

For now, this ends this part of my journey with gemstones, but the adventure continues. Who knows what new and amazing discoveries will be made in the future? Time will tell.

Part 3

Healing with the Stones

Forty-One
Discovering the Spiritual Bodies

In Part 1 we talked about the three energetic layers of human beings: the astral, mental and causal bodies.

When we engage in gemstone healing, particularly when we are performing this process on others, it is important that we begin to notice the existence of the subtle energy system.

I teach the ancient Japanese healing art of Reiki. In my class, one of the first things students must learn is how to scan the body and to sense each other's three-layered energetic system. We also scan to see if each of the seven main chakra centers is fully open and functioning. In Reiki, we do this by using our own senses and our hands.

Before you begin the process, have your partner lie down on the floor, bed or massage table. Try to imagine you can feel each of the three layers of your subject's energetic field.

Stretch your arms as high as they will go, then make your hands parallel to the body. Keep your hands flat and high in the air over your partner's body. Close your eyes if you need to; it may help you to feel the energy easier.

Now, let your hands "fall" slowly down toward the body, until you can feel a place where the energy seems a bit denser. You should feel this about 18 inches to two feet above your subject's body. Stop there and run your hands horizontally along this line. You may begin to feel a slight tingling sensation in your hands.

Can you feel it? This is your partner's causal, or spiritual, body. If not, keep trying! It will happen, believe me!

Next, let your hands fall some more until they get about six to eight inches above your partner. You should begin to feel another dense energy pattern. It will feel as if the energy has shifted and, perhaps, become denser than that of the previous field. Can you feel that one? It is the mental body, the place from which we manifest.

Finally, allow your hands to fall to a point one to two inches above your partner's body, and you will feel their astral layer. Run your hands horizontally over your partner again to feel this entire layer of energy. Chances are good this layer will be the densest of the three, since it is closest to the body.

Please don't be discouraged if you find you cannot sense this right away-keep working with it! I promise that if you set your intent, it will happen eventually.

The Pendulum

Next, we must be able to sense the seven major chakra centers of the body. I use the term "major" because there are actually hundreds of lesser energetic centers in and around the human body. Many are actually present in our etheric, or hologram, body. For basic, day-to-day health concerns, though, we are concerned with the seven major centers discussed briefly in the first part of the book.

Sensing the chakras and being able to determine whether they are properly functioning seems to be more difficult, even for me at times, and I have been practicing for several years. When new gemstone healing students begin class, I have found it is often easier to initially use a tool to do this as we slowly open ourselves to feeling these energetic systems.

The pendulum is a great tool to use for detecting energetic fields. A pendulum is usually a point of some sort attached to a chain or string. For centuries, pendulum-like devices have been used for such purposes as dowsing to find water or precious metals. Pendulums are now commonly used by modern-day psychics as a tool for directing the unconscious mind to receive information.

To use the pendulum to scan someone's auric field, simply begin with the subject lying down face up. Run the pendulum over his or her body to see if the centers are open.

At the beginning of the book, I mentioned that the chakras are like little funnel clouds that swirl in various directions. To see if they are open, place the pendulum about two inches above your subject's body. Beginning at the feet, slowly walk with the pendulum up the body without swinging it back and forth. You will find it begins to move on its own as you pass each chakra center.

Students really get excited when they see this happen for the first time-they are astounded that the pendulum really moves on its own from the energy given off by the body! I can understand that-it still amazes me.

If properly functioning, the three lower chakras should be moving in a counterclockwise direction, so the pendulum should do likewise. As you approach the area between the knees, you should begin to sense the root chakra because it moves down toward the earth and the feet. Continue moving up the body toward the head, keeping the pendulum an inch above the body. Take care to watch for blockages in any of the seven main chakra centers.

The sacral, or second, chakra is located just below the navel; the solar plexus, or third chakra, is located in the area where the ribs meet in the center of your body. Keep moving up the body. Under normal circumstances, the pendulum should rotate in a circular, counterclockwise motion.

As you slowly move toward the heart center, you should begin to see the pendulum shift and to rotate in the opposite direction, meaning it will now be swinging clockwise.

Next go to the throat, then to the third eye (located on your forehead). Finally, place the pendulum above the person's head. As you do this, you should notice the pendulum moving, which would indicate that the chakra is open and functioning.

You may observe that the pendulum moves more at some chakra centers than at others. This could indicate a slight blockage in the areas where it does not move as well.

What if this is not working at all?

If you are doing the process I have described above and nothing is happening, do not worry! There are a couple of reasons why this can occur.

You may simply need to spend more time working with the pendulum itself. One good way to do this is to hold the pendulum and ask it a simple yes or no question it can easily answer, such as, "Is my name _____?" Then, allow it to give you a "yes" signal. Likewise, ask the pendulum a question it can easily say no to and allow it to give you a "no" signal.

The "yes" should swing in one direction, the "no" in another. By working with the pendulum this way, you are developing a rapport with your unconscious mind-the part of you that works the pendulum.

After practicing for a while, you should start seeing some results. Then you can try the body scan again to see if you can sense the seven chakra centers.

If it still does not work, there is a distinct possibility that the person you're working with is extremely blocked. This is not a judgment of your subject; the poor soul may simply be so stressed out that their chakras are blocked.

The most stunning example I've ever seen of stress and its effect on the chakra system happened at my office about a year ago, when a woman came to me for energy work. She had recently lost her job and was at the end of her rope, so to speak.

I started the session by scanning her energy field, using the method I shared with you. Then, I began attempting to sense the seven chakras using my hands. To my surprise, I felt nothing.

Of course, I immediately began wondering what was wrong with me that I could not get a sense of this woman's energy field. Either I was totally losing it, or the poor thing was completely shut down. I decided to take out the pendulum to check it out.

Sure enough, every single chakra was completely blocked! It was amazing! I have never seen that before or since.

My goal for the session then became to simply unblock the system and to get it flowing again. The technique I used is something you can use on everyone, but it is particularly helpful to those who may be suffering from blockages.

Forty-Two
Laying-on-of-Stones

So at that point, I began to do what you will always do when giving a stone treatment: I began to run a chunk of Amethyst above her body from head to toe and through her three energetic layers.

This process removes energetic blockages from the auric field, and Amethyst is one of the best stones I know of for doing that!

In the case of the extremely stressed out woman, I had to do it for quite a while and strongly focus my intent on clearing any blockages prohibiting the proper functioning of the chakra system. I did this until I intuitively knew that progress had been made. Then I proceeded to do what I will now teach you how to do: place the stones on the physical body.

I use seven stones, one for each chakra, when I teach my basic class. I use the following:

Hematite for the root, Red Jasper for the sacral, Citrine for the solar plexus, Rose Quartz for the heart, Sodalite for the throat, Amethyst for the third eye, and clear Quartz crystal for the crown.

For reference, you may look at the chart provided in the first section of the book for exact placement. Simply look at the chart and place the stones accordingly, with the proper stone on its corresponding chakra center.

Afterwards, I proceeded to use different forms of energy work, such as Reiki, on her. The stones can act as an extremely powerful amplifier to the energy you are sending to your subject.

Even if you have no formal training in energy balancing, though, the stones will do their job. As they lay on your subject's chakra centers, I suggest you continue to run a chunk of Amethyst over the three layers of the body discussed earlier.

Intuition will tell you when it is time to end and/or to turn the subject over. Most of my sessions run for one hour, so I work a half hour on each side.

Sometimes, though, the healing may take longer. Always rely on your intuitive guidance-it will let you know what the person needs. Certain injured or ill areas may require longer periods of time. Most of you who are reading this will usually be working on family members and close friends, at least at first. Therefore, time is not really a factor; it is more important that you pay attention to those areas that need more attention and to work on those.

If and when you feel it to be appropriate, turn your subject over and work on the back. Place the stones in their proper locations and, again, begin to run the Amethyst over their subtle energy bodies. When you turn someone over, be sure to remember that their heart is then on the opposite side! I still have to think about that so I don't put the stone on the wrong side of the chest!

I believe it is critical to work on a person's back. As I have said throughout, thoughts are actual things that occupy space. It is my opinion, and that of many other energy healers, that you store your karma on your back. This means that there is an energetic component to your past lives, and those energetic patterns are often stuck in the auric field surrounding your back. That's why I believe it is so important to clear this area whenever possible. So, whenever possible, turn your subject over and have him or her lie with the stones on the back. It is very powerful.

Self-Healing

During self-healing sessions, I often lay down and place the stones directly on each of my chakra centers or anywhere I feel intuitively guided to place a stone.

There is a distinct sensation you will feel as you lie still. It is like a rush of energy. At first, you will feel nothing at all, but if you are patient, about ten to fifteen minutes into your "power nap," as I like to call it, you will begin to get an amazing feeling as the energetic vibrations of the stones begin to work magic on you.

It is like a huge rush and then it calms down, usually after twenty minutes or so. When that happens, you can gently remove the stones and get on with your day feeling refreshed and rejuvenated.

Meditations with Gemstones

I recommend experimenting with different stones in meditation. They are powerful tools to allow your subconscious mind to tune into whatever you need at that particular time. Pay attention to which stone you are attracted to as well. It can give clues as to your true inner self.

Gem Meditation

The following is an easy, fun exercise for you to try at home.

First, pick out your favorite stone, or the stone you are intuitively guided to use at this time. For purposes of this exercise, I will refer to it as Smoky Quartz because it is one of my favorites to do this with.

Find a comfortable spot to sit down, holding the piece of Smoky Quartz in your hands. Close your eyes.

Now begin to imagine the feeling of the Smoky Quartz. Is it cool? Warm? Light? Heavy? Just begin to allow yourself to tune into the stone at this time.

Now imagine that the Smoky Quartz could expand and become bigger and bigger. See, feel or imagine it surrounding your entire body. Feel as if you are floating inside the giant piece of Smoky Quartz. Allow it to create a bubble around your body at least 3 feet in diameter.

Float inside the Smoky Quartz. How does it feel? Imagine you can feel the golden brown light of the crystal as it heals you and protects you.

Can you feel it? Great!

Now imagine that inside this protective shell only that which is for your highest good can get through.

Imagine that you are totally safe and protected energetically from all negativity.

You are surrounded by the healing loving energies of Smoky Quartz.

Allow that love to permeate your entire being. Imagine that you are surrounded by this protective shell and that anything sent to you will be transmuted into love and light and sent back to those who sent it.

Continue to become one with the stone. Feel the grounding energies as Smoky Quartz connects you with Mother Earth. Imagine you are totally grounded, centered and balanced now.

When you are ready, begin to imagine the Smoky Quartz bubble drawing close to you as if you could take it with you today to all of your activities.

Now begin to return your focus to the stone in your hand, knowing that you are taking that protective energy with you as you venture out into the world.

When you are ready, open your eyes and come back into the room feeling wide awake and refreshed!

One thing I like to remind people of when trying exercises like these at home is that you can make an audio tape of yourself reading the steps from the book. This is very effective because, as I said in my last book, your unconscious mind loves to hear the sound of your voice.

This may seem tough to do, but believe me, it only takes a minute and makes the process go smoothly so you can try it whenever you wish.

The Big Picture

People have often asked me why a hypnotherapist would be so concerned about learning and doing energy work in conjunction with a hypnotherapy practice. To many, the two seem totally unrelated .

In my work, I have discovered I can take a person into the past verbally and allow them to see patterns and heal past lives. This is good, but the effectiveness of the process quadruples when hypnotherapy is combined with energy work.

For every lifetime that is consciously revisited and healed, there is a corresponding energetic component that resides somewhere in the auric field. To get the most out of the process, the energetic component must be healed as well through energy work.

We store memories of our past lives around our bodies holographically. This may seem a bit far out, but it's true! So when someone comes in to see me, I want to make sure I can address the situation at both a subconscious and an energetic level to achieve the best results.

As I have progressed in my practice, my work now includes the use of sacred sounds that can simultaneously address the subconscious while instantaneously clearing energetic blockages. Again, using the crystals and gemstones in that process serves as an amplifier to facilitate the healing.

I plan to explore that more in greater detail in the future.

Forty-Three
Conclusion

Many theorists of the New Age believe that planet Earth is currently going through a vibrational shift to a higher frequency. That drastic change in energy is difficult for many people to handle.

This is why, in my opinion, we are beginning to see diseases affecting the nervous system such as Parkinson's, Super Nuclear Palsy, Alzheimer's and others creep up on the population.

I believe that all vibrational medicine assists the physical body in transcending gracefully to higher vibrations so we may thrive and function in the coming years. I hope this book has shed some light on the subject to inspire people to look into it in greater depth.

So here I must answer the question I posed at the beginning of this exploration in healing: Do gemstones actually heal, or are they merely a focal point for our unconscious mind?

I believe the answer is both.

There is no doubt that we are all affected by energies around us, so it would be naive to say that stones and crystals are not a significant part of that.

On the other hand, gazing into a stunning creation of nature is certainly one way to shift our attention away from the mundane and into the realm of infinite possibilities.

We were all born with the God given ability to heal ourselves and others. I believe we only need to be shown the part of ourselves we had forgotten, so we may remember our inborn gifts.

Glossary

Astral Body - a part of the subtle energy system. The energetic layer closest to the physical body.

Blueprint -see etheric double

Causal Body - a part of the subtle energy system. The layer farthest from the physical body associated with spirituality.

Chakra - one of seven energy centers in the human body identified by Eastern philosophy.

> **Crown Chakra -** the seventh energy center vibrating to a white color frequency located at the top of the head is the spiritual center of a person.

Third Eye chakra - The sixth energy center located at the brow deals with intuition and psychic abilities. Vibrates to an indigo color.

Throat chakra - the fifth energy center vibrating to a light blue color deals with communication.

Heart chakra - the fourth energy center vibrates to the color green is the center of the soul.

Solar Plexus chakra - The third energy center in a person deals with power and boundaries and vibrates to a yellow color frequency.

Sacral chakra - the second energy center in a person vibrating to the color orange deals with sexuality and creativity.

Root chakra - the first energy center vibrating to a red frequency deal with issues of survival and grounding.

Clairaudience - the ability to hear the dead, or to perceive sounds without actually hearing them with the ears.

Clairsentience - Perceiving thoughts that are coming from outside yourself.

Clairvoyance - the ability to see the future, or to perceive things that cannot be seen.

Collective consciousness - concept developed by Carl Jung used to describe the phenomena of the mass thoughts of our society.

Crystal - occurs when atoms are uniformly placed in a solid structure and the pattern repeats itself in three dimensions.

Dharma - Sanskrit word meaning "purpose in life."

Etheric double - the holographic image of a person in a state of wholeness and perfection also known as the etheric blueprint.

Gemstone - a rock or mineral unique because of its beauty.

Karma - the concept that for every action there is a reaction. You reap what you sow.

Matrix - fine grain section of a rock. The sedimentary layers of minerals that form between gemstones.

Mental Body - one of the spiritual bodies of a person that deals with issues of manifestation and abundance.

Mineral - an inorganic piece of the Earth's crust that can be identified by a chemical composition, a solid crystalline substance.

Psychic attack - the effects of negative thoughts on a person's energetic center.

Rock - the result of one or more minerals combining to form a mass of sometimes non-crystalline structures.

Stone - term for any part of the earth's crust with the exception of ice and coal.

Thoughtform - the concept that thoughts are things which occupy space.

Bibliography

Andrews, Shirley. <u>Atlantis: Insights From a Lost Civilization</u>. St. Paul, MN: Llewellyn Publications, 1997.

Andrews, Ted. <u>How to Heal with Color.</u> St. Paul, MN: Llewellyn Publications, 1993.

Andrews, Ted. <u>How to See and Read the Aura</u>. St. Paul, MN: Llewellyn Publications, 2001.

Angelo, Jack. <u>Spiritual Healing: Energy Medicine for Health and Well-Being</u>. Boston, MA: Element Books Limited, 1991.

Bonewitz, Ra. <u>The Cosmic Crystal Spiral</u>. Great Britain: Element Books Ltd., 1986.

Cayce, Edgar Evans. <u>Atlantis</u>. New York, NY: St. Martin's Paperbacks, 1988.

Cayce, Edgar Evans. <u>Mysteries of Atlantis Revisited</u>. New York, NY: St. Martin's Paperbacks, 1988.

Chopra, Deepak. <u>Quantum Healing: Exploring the Frontiers of Mind/Body Medicine</u>. New York, NY: Bantam Books, 1989.

Chopra, Deepak. <u>The Seven Spiritual Laws of Success.</u> San Rafael, CA: Amber-Allen Publishing, 1994.

Choquette, Sonja. <u>Psychic Pathways</u>. New York: NY: Three Rivers Press, 1994.

Cunningham, Scott. <u>Cunningham's Encyclopedia of Crystal Gem and Metal Magic</u>. St. Paul, MN: Llewellyn Publications, 1988.

Cunningham, Scott. <u>Earth Air Fire and Water</u>. St. Paul, MN: Llewellyn Publications, 1991.

Cunningham, Scott. <u>Magical Aromatherapy</u>. St. Paul, MN: Llewellyn Publications, 1989.

Cunningham, Scott. <u>Magical Household</u>. St. Paul, MN: Llewellyn Publications, 1983.

Cunningham, Scott. <u>Wicca: A Guide for the Solitary Practitioner.</u> St. Paul, MN: Llewellyn Publications, 1988.

Darling, Wayne "Lone Eagle." <u>Fifth Dimensional Healing: Crystal Wizdom and the Five Elements of Multidimensional Healing</u>. Canada: Wizdom Books, 1999.

Doreal, M. <u>Astral Projection and How to Accomplish It</u>. Castle Rock, CO: Brotherhood of the White Temple, Inc., 1992.

Gerber, Richard. <u>Vibrational Healing</u>. Santa Fe, NM: Bear & Company, 1988.

Goldschneider, Gary. <u>The Secret Language of Birthdays: Personology Profiles for Each Day of the Year.</u> New York, NY: Penguin Studio, 1994.

Gordon, Richard. <u>Quantum-Touch: The Power to Heal.</u> North Atlantic Books: Berkeley, CA, 1999.

"Jung, Carl (Gustav)." The New Encyclopaedia Britannica: Macropaedia. 15th ed. Chicago: University Press, 1975.

Katz, Michael. Gemisphere Luminary. Portland, OR: Gemiphere, 1997.

Melody. Love is in the Earth. Wheatridge, CO: Earth-Love Publishing House, 1995.

Melody. Laying-On-of-Stones. Wheatridge, CO: Earth-Love Publishing House, 1992.

Myss, Carolyn. Anatomy of the Spirit. New York: NY: Three Rivers Press, 1996.

Myss Carolyn. Sacred Contracts. New York: NY: Harmony Books, 2001.

Prinz, Martin. Simon & Schuster's Guide to Rocks and Minerals. Spain: Fireside Books: 1977.

Rand, William Lee. Reiki: The Healing Touch. Southfield, MI: Vision Publications, 1998.

Raphaell, Katrina. Crystal Enlightenment. Santa Fe, NM: Aurora Press, Inc. 1985.

Schiegl, Heinz. <u>Healing Magnetism.</u> York Beach, Maine: Samuel Weiser, Inc., 1987.

Schumann, Walter. <u>Gemstones of the World</u>. New York: Sterling Publishing Co., Inc., 1997.

Sherwood, Keith. <u>Chakra Therapy</u>. St. Paul, MN: Llewellyn Publications, 1988.

Slate, Joe, Ph.D. <u>Psychic Vampires</u>. St. Paul, MN: Llewellyn Publications, 2002.

Stein, Diane. <u>Essential Reiki.</u> Freedom, CA: The Crossing Press, Inc. 1995.

Stone, Robert B., Ph.D. <u>The Secret Life of Your Cells</u>. Atglen, PA: Whitford Press, 1989.

Vennels, David F. <u>Bach Flower Remedies for Beginners</u>. St. Paul, MN: Llewellyn Publications, 2001.

Wauters, Ambika. <u>Chakras and Their Archetypes: Uniting Energy Awareness and Spiritual Growth.</u> Freedom, CA: The Crossing Press, 1997.

Index